Getting it Together

Getting it Together

Spiritual Practices for Faith, Family, and Work

Carol A. Wehrheim

Westminster John Knox Press
LOUISVILLE • LONDON

Cover design by Rohani Design
Cover art © Fiona Frank/Allsport/Getty Images

First edition
Published by Westminster John Knox Press
Louisville, Kentucky

This book is printed on acid-free paper that meets the American National Standards Institute Z39.48 standard. ♾

PRINTED IN THE UNITED STATES OF AMERICA

04 05 06 07 08 09 10 11 — 10 9 8 7 6 5 4 3 2

Library of Congress Cataloging-in-Publication Data

Wehrheim, Carol A.
    Getting it together : spiritual practices for faith, family, and work / Carol A. Wehrheim.
        p. cm.
    Includes bibliographical references.
    ISBN 0-664-22582-9 (alk. paper)
    1. Christian life. 2. Spiritual life. I. Title.

BV4501.3 .W42 2002
248.4—dc21

2002071452

Contents

Introduction		1
Chapter 1	The Foundation of Your Life	5
Chapter 2	Not Enough Time, Too Many Choices	15
Chapter 3	Moving Ahead	24
Chapter 4	Creative Problem Solving	33
Chapter 5	Keep On Keeping On	42
Leader's Guide		49
Introduction		51
Session 1	The Foundation of Your Life	57
Session 2	Not Enough Time, Too Many Choices	69
Session 3	Moving Ahead	80
Session 4	Creative Problem Solving	91
Session 5	Keep On Keeping On	104
Notes		117
Bibliography		119

Introduction

The Williams family, parents Carlos and Jane with their children Maria (8) and Richard (13), live in a midsized city. They are active in their church, attending worship regularly, helping in mission projects, and serving in leadership roles. Both parents are employed full-time, and the children attend nearby public schools.

Three women—Jennie, Martha, and Esther—knew one another previously but became good friends when they attended the same program sponsored by their church on how to live more faithfully. All belong to a large congregation, and all are employed full-time, though Jennie will retire in another year. Martha is the youngest of the three by ten or twelve years. Esther moved to the area a year or so before the church program, while the other two women have lived there most of their lives. They have dinner together at least once a month to talk about their faith and how they are progressing in desired changes in their individual and communal lives.

You will get to know the people described above as you read this book and as they progress through the process suggested here. Like many people, they face the problem of numerous competing claims on their time. Before we learn more about them, however, let's set the stage.

What's the Big Picture?

Before the industrial revolution about two hundred years ago, most families worked side by side, juggling work and family tasks. When men and women began to leave their farm or family business for factories or other places of work, a significant change occurred. In those families where it was possible, the mother stayed home to care for the children and keep house. The men were now the breadwinners, at least for the middle class. This continued to be the desired image, if not always the reality, although the number of working women with school-age children continued to grow.

By 1990, 53 percent of women with preschool children worked, and 66 percent of all mothers worked. For various reasons, from economic need to personal fulfillment, these numbers are not likely to change, and are especially not likely to drop, in the near future. This reality alone might prompt many families to search for ways to balance the personal, work, and church responsibilities they have.

The number of mothers working outside the home is not, however, the only reason that adults today—married and single, parents or not—feel the tension of competing interests and disappearing time. In the 1960s, church leaders talked eagerly of the years ahead when we would all enjoy more leisure time, time to pursue hobbies and intellectual interests as well as to participate in the ministries of our faith communities. Now, near the end of the century, where has that promised leisure time gone?

While technology has provided much to help us in the workplace and at home, it has also increased the pace of our lives. Airmail has given way to e-mail. Answering services and answering machines have become too slow for us, and we have cell phones and pagers so we are never out of reach. A manuscript can be sent to the editor overnight by modem, and the requests for the rewrite are back before you have a chance to take a deep breath. We have little or no "down" time.

For most people, the changes in the workplace add even more pressure. We looked forward to shorter work weeks two or three decades ago, but the average worker in the United States now works significantly more hours than in 1960. If you are not on a career track where a 70-hour week is considered normal, you may be working two or three jobs to pay the bills. Researchers say that many of us suffer from chronic fatigue because, with the increased demands on our time, we sleep too little.

All these factors, along with the stress of life in an age when we know within hours of violence, tragedy, and humanitarian crises in our community and around the globe, put tremendous pressure on adults and children today. We may find ourselves responsible for our parents as well as our children. Whether *you* are in such a bind is not really the issue; for when *others* are, the quality of life for all of us suffers. As Paul wrote to the church in Corinth, "If one member suffers, all suffer together with it" (1 Cor. 12:26).

More Than a Woman's Problem

Articles appear regularly in magazines and newspapers that describe the difficulty of working and raising a family. Usually the articles are directed to women. They may give tips on how to be a "supermom" or say that "you can't have it all." In truth, however, this is not just a woman's problem. People of all ages, genders, career paths, and family situations are caught in the web of competing responsibilities for family, work, and self. For people of faith, these responsibilities, as well as ministry to others, face us daily.

A few conversations with single adults and married couples without children quickly alert you to the stress they are experiencing as well. The grocery store checkout clerk who must care for a parent with Alzheimer's disease is just as affected as the dual-career family trying to find a live-in nanny for their children. The choices we must make daily keep stress high and cause us great anxiety. It doesn't help that many of the causes of this stress and anxiety are out of our hands.

The Foundation of Our Life

This book is written specifically for Christians and begins with the assumption that, whatever our situation, we must begin by building a firm foundation of faith. The struggle to maintain a balanced life, a life of creative rather than destructive tension, will always be with us. To live with that tension, we are wise if we make time for growing with God our priority. This book is designed to help you make time with God productive through Bible study and specific spiritual disciplines.

Each chapter begins with a selection from Scripture and some words about the passage. You are encouraged to ponder the meaning of the passage for your life today. Take time to read the Bible passage before continuing.

At the conclusion of each chapter is a spiritual discipline. Spiritual disciplines are activities that nurture our spiritual life. While there are many definitions of spirituality today, this book defines it as "the way we choose to live out our faith."[1] Spiritual disciplines or practices help us nurture our faith and grow in our relationship with God. They are essential to a vibrant faith, a faith that will sustain us in this tense, hurried world. Of the many types of spiritual disciplines, five are described in these chapters. Practice each one before you continue to read. Each was chosen to complement that particular chapter.

How to Use This Book

This book consists of five chapters for participants followed by five session guides for a group leader. If you are in a group, your leader will assign the chapters for you to read. If you are not in a group, you might take several weeks to read all five chapters, spacing the reading to give you time to practice some of the suggestions. Try keeping a journal of your experiences and what you are trying. This is particularly helpful if you have no one with whom to discuss your reading, questions, and ideas.

If you are a group leader, be sure to read the participant's chapters as well as the leader's guide for each session.

If you have a spouse or partner, read the book together. Talk about the ideas. Plan ways to try the process. While this is not exactly a how-to book, reading the book without living it is a bit like reading a book on praying but never trying to pray. If you are single or are reading this book on your own, find a friend to discuss it with you. Living faithfully is not something we do alone.

Chapter One
The Foundation of Your Life

Carlos and Jane Williams are seated at their kitchen table. They are discussing the values that they want their children to understand as important for their family. While they have had no particular trouble with their children, recent articles and news stories about children across the country acting violently against other children have raised their awareness of values education. What Christian values are they passing on to their children?

Carlos and Jane are also disturbed about the expectations of some of their children's friends, particularly the assumption that they can have all the things that a materialistic culture can provide. Just last night, their daughter Maria ran to her room crying when she was told that she could not have a particular designer-brand sweater because she already had a similar sweater that was still quite wearable. The Williamses are trying to figure out how to discuss faith and values with their children. In the process, they have discovered that they have not talked about these matters recently and have some serious discussions ahead of them.

Jennie, Martha, and Esther have talked about many things since they worked together during the church program on living faithfully. Now the trust among them is so strong that any one of them can bring a difficulty to the group and know that it will be discussed fairly and confidentially. Tonight Jennie has the floor. She will retire in a few months and is wondering how to look at retirement homes, even though she does not expect to move from her own home for several years. Because she has heard horrendous stories about waiting lists, she wants to begin her search soon.

Esther raises a question about proximity to their church or another faith community. Martha asks about volunteer opportunities. Both women know that Jennie has already checked her finances, but they want to help her examine some less obvious issues. Values, faith, commitments and more are woven into their conversation. Jennie is grateful for their help, but now she has a lot of thinking to do. Their questions open up areas that she has not even imagined until now.

So what about you? You probably identified with some of the descriptions and statistics in the introduction.

Now you can consider some of the pieces of your life and how to balance it to better advantage for you and all concerned. Which of your values are so important to you that you would want them to be passed to your children, your grandchildren, nieces, nephews, or any of the next generation? What values are central to the major decisions facing you? What does it mean to live faithfully in this fast-paced and changing world?

One way to think about how to reshape your life is to turn to Scripture. Read Deuteronomy 32:44–47 and Micah 6:6–8. What phrases there leap out at you, drawing you to ponder them more deeply? Why did those phrases attract you? What meaning do these verses have for you today?

Deuteronomy 32:44–47

In Deuteronomy 32, Moses was preparing to die. God had told him that he would not be allowed to enter Canaan. Instead, the Israelites would be led to the Promised Land by Joshua. The book of Deuteronomy contains Moses' final addresses to this people called by God. A few verses of special importance for our reading are near the end of these speeches: "Take to heart all the words that I am giving in witness against you today; give them as a command to your children, so that they may diligently observe all the words of the law. This is no trifling matter for you, but rather your very life; through it you may live long in the land that you are crossing over the Jordan to possess." Then Moses pronounced blessings on each tribe before he died. He was buried and the mantle of leadership passed to Joshua, whom Moses had trained as his successor.

Patrick Miller, in his commentary on Deuteronomy, links these verses with those in 34:1–12, recognizing that the death of Moses began a new era for God's people.[1] However, what Moses, a mortal who spoke face to face with God, gave them was the Torah, the promise and the instruction by which they were to live thereafter. It is this Torah that the people were and are, even today, to pass on to the next generations.

Moses did not single out parents for these words but was addressing all the adults. We are all responsible for nurturing the next generation in faith. This same concept of communal responsibility is evident in the New Testament. Little is said about family in the New Testament, but entire households are converted and baptized. We continue this emphasis today. When we dedicate or baptize infants, we take on the corporate responsibility of nurturing these children in the faith. These rituals recognize that this task is important and that we must all be involved. To paraphrase an African saying, it takes a congregation to raise a child in the faith. Whether or not you are a parent, Moses had you in mind.

The Torah is not only a set of rules, for God's promise is behind the instruction that Moses tells them and us to remember. God's steadfast love is what makes these laws not only important but also, as Moses says, "our very life." Today, Christians would do well to heed Moses' admonition, for God's promise and Word are to us too our very life.

Micah 6:6–8

Even as some commentators call Deuteronomy the most important book of the Old Testament or Hebrew Scriptures for understanding the New Testament, the verse that best summarizes the prophetic teachings, and perhaps even these final addresses of Moses, is Micah 6:8. Even with God's word firmly in us, we must still ask what God requires of us. The prophet answers the question about as succinctly as it can be said: "To do justice, and to love kindness, and to walk humbly with your God" (Mic. 6:8).

These two Hebrew Scriptures passages are the framework against which we struggle with our values and faith today. We know that God has promised to provide us with all that we need. We recall the words of God to Zechariah, "Not by might, not by power, but by my spirit" (Zech. 4:6), and are confident that with God's Spirit we can do what God calls us to do. Alongside that promise we must continually ask, "What does God require of us in this time and place?" For ourselves, we ask, "What are the values and what is the faith that I lean on from day to day? What are the promise and instruction that were taught to me, ingrained in me so deeply that I may even act without bringing them to the fore?" Then come the questions that may have prompted you to pick up this book: "How do I manage all the parts of my life to live as God calls me to live?

How do I achieve a balance? How do I impart this faith and these values to my children, all children?"

The Commitments That Uphold Us

As we noted in the introduction, the act of balancing our responsibilities to ourselves, our family, our work, and our church is one that challenges every adult, whatever her or his household arrangement. When we try to live without taking into account our connectedness, whether as individuals or as a family unit, we are doomed to failure. Certainly we in the Christian church should understand this. We come together for prayer, worship, study, and fellowship. We recognize that while parents may be the primary role models for nurturing their children's faith, the whole congregation shares in that task. We recall that role through promises made by the congregation at an infant baptism or dedication or by acknowledging the special role of godparents for the young child. However, we minister to one another throughout our lives, giving care, comforting, and rejoicing together.

We all make decisions, thoughtfully or hastily, on the values and commitments that have become a deep part of us. Sometimes these commitments are so thoroughly ingrained in us that we hardly know we have drawn on them, as we decide where to vacation or how our children ought to behave in public. Some of us tested those values given us by our parents in our adolescent or early adulthood years, found them wanting, and took on new values, even trying out several types. Others of us simply took on the mantle of faith values we were given, never questioning whether this mantle was the one we could really call our own. Changes in the culture around us often call our commitments into question, even though we may try to avoid this confrontation.

In order to find a better balance for more faithful living, we will need to dig down within ourselves to discover the commitments and values that are most important to us. We may find that some values are no longer important. We may find that some are hidden so deeply that we had forgotten about them.

Where Do Our Commitments Come From?

The commitments that actually determine our choices may have come to us through subtle messages from our families, parents and grandparents, aunts and uncles. For example, the women in one family may have been busy all day long—cooking, caring for children, sewing in their spare time. Hands were always active. Even with the labor-saving devices of today, this generation's women in that family find it hard to sit idly as they watch television. The message they got was that you can always be doing something constructive. Sitting with your hands folded may lead to anything from doing the work of the devil to leaving tasks not done.

The boy who has never seen a man

in his family help out in the kitchen grows up assuming that kitchen tasks are women's work. That young man, who cooks for himself when living alone, forgets how to boil water when he is married! That message was never stated, but the learning was clear and deep. For that family, kitchen work is not for the men.

In still another family, no non-essential work was performed on Sunday. While the neighbors on one side of them routinely washed their cars on Sunday afternoon and those on the other side cleaned the house, this family played games together and visited friends and family members after attending church in the morning.

What are the values that you live by? Take a few minutes to write down what is most important to you. You can approach this in a variety of ways. Begin by answering one of these questions:

1. How do you spend your time during most weeks? Look at your calendar. What areas of your life garner the most hours? What happens to the hours that are yours to use as you wish?

2. How do you budget your money? Get out your checkbook. Frequently the way we spend our money says what is most important to us. Which bills get paid first? What commands the majority of your expendable money?

3. Who are your friends? Who are the people you meet in your workplace, at the church, in your neighborhood, your family members? In what ways do you value these people? What do your interactions tell you about the values you hold?

4. What sayings or slogans do you use frequently? These may be sayings that you grew up with, or they may be some you acquired along the way. You may even say them jokingly, but upon closer examination you recognize that they represent what you hold important.

5. How do you make decisions? Consider decisions—minor and major ones—you have made within the last few months. What values and commitments did they express?

Once you have made a list of your values and commitments, try to group or sort them by category. Perhaps several are connected to family matters, while others have to do with work habits. Keep this list around for a couple days, adding to it as you recognize the values and commitments that come into play as you move through each day. Reflect on the passages from Deuteronomy and Micah. What commitments important to you are suggested by these ancient words?

The Role of Success

Another way to consider what is important to you is to reflect on this question: What defines success for me? You might answer this question by recalling a time when you felt successful or thinking about what would make you feel successful today. Look back over your life. What was success when you were a teenager? What was success as you began your adult life? How has your idea of success changed over these years? Did it change when you became a parent or when you knew you would not be a parent?

Once you have answered the question about success, compare the values you determined to be important for you with your definition of success. Do they fit together comfortably, or is there a clash between them? Do your commitments and values undergird your sense of success, or do your values challenge your sense of success? In other words, does your image of success match your understanding of living faithfully?

The Importance of Our Commitments

Core faith values are the foundation for how you live your life. They represent your faith in action, your belief system on parade. They are the basis on which you make decisions about how you perform your responsibilities for your family, your work, your faith community, and yourself. In the rush of daily life, these values are left by the wayside more often than we would like. When that happens, we begin to feel lopsided and out of kilter. As Scott Peck says, "Balancing is the discipline that gives us flexibility. Extraordinary flexibility is required for successful living in all spheres of activity. . . . The loss of balance is ultimately more painful than the giving up required to maintain balance."[2]

Where is the imbalance between your daily life and the commitments you want to live? As parents and family members, we may see the imbalance most clearly when we compare what we want to teach our children with the values that control our day-to-day existence. Frequently, our children point these imbalances out to us. While the Williams children did not do so openly, Carlos and Jane began to wonder about the standards they lived by because of their children's actions. But the imbalance is not always caused by a problem. Jennie will live with imbalance when she retires until she finds the right creative tension for her to live faithfully.

The tensions in our lives created by the loss of balance are usually harder for us to accept than the changes required to regain that balance. To rebalance, we have to spend time examining our faith commitments and values and how they fit together. The purpose of this book is to help you examine your faith and commitments and determine better ways to live them so that your life exemplifies them, so that your life is once more in balance.

Commitments + Life = Mission Statement

When we do not examine our commitments from time to time, particularly as our lives or family configurations change, we miss a wonderful opportunity to get our lives back in balance and to develop our spiritual life as well. As we age, as our children mature, as we move ahead in a career, we have another chance to set our lives aright, to recognize God's presence with us. This may be the point for Jennie as she ponders what retirement will mean for her, especially for her understanding of her own self-worth and success. Her friends can be most helpful at this time as they affirm her as an individual of worth and a child of God.

Once we have decided that we do indeed want to expend energy and time building a more faithful life, a life that balances our various responsibilities, one way to begin is by writing a mission statement. You may have participated in a similar project with your congregation or even with your business, though for different reasons. In theological language, you are accepting your call from God and seeking to discern your vocation today, for vocation can change over one's lifetime.

Why a mission statement for families and groups of Christian friends? Diana R. Garland pursues this question as she reflects on the creation story in Genesis 2:7–3:13.[3] We have forgotten that God gave Adam work in the garden of Eden, she says. Adam was to till the soil and keep the garden. Eve was to be a partner in that work. Instead, the two of them (note that Adam was with Eve according to Genesis 3:6) were more interested in the forbidden tree than in tilling and weeding. Garland contends that the problem here is not so much that Adam and Eve ate the fruit, but that they had forgotten the purpose of their partnership, the purpose of their ministry in the garden. In short, they ignored their family mission statement, the mission given them by God, their creator.

From this basis, she says that families are to do something more than give support to one another. While each family has to learn to live together justly and lovingly, each one needs also to determine what their ministry is and what their partnership is called to do. The family is an important place where children are nurtured in the faith. The ways we care for our children and for others speaks volumes about the love of God. Might your mission be found in the inner city or in a hospital? Might it be taking in foster children or freeing others to participate in a special mission project? The possibilities are endless, but each family or group needs to be specific about how they will enter into mission.

Although you are probably reading this book by yourself, a mission statement cannot really be written in isolation. If you are part of a family, the family must be included. If you are single, look for a few friends who share your commitments and faith and write a statement together. Then you will have others to help you remain accountable to your calling.

Of course, your mission statement will change as your life and family circumstances change. For example, a single parent with an eight-year-old child might have this mission statement: *To broaden our family circle, we seek opportunities to invite older adults to our home and we work with our church in mission projects.* A family of two parents and two adolescent children might see their mission as this: *As a family we live our faith openly by participating in mission projects together.* And parents, take note. Whatever the age of your children, when you participate in mission together, you are educating them about the Christian life and nurturing them in the way of the faithful.

Three adults from the same congregation, such as Jennie, Martha, and Esther, might write this mission statement for themselves: *While we continue to help one another discern God's will for our individual lives, we will also come together to practice the spiritual discipline of hospitality.*

You may incorporate others into your family as partners in your mission as well. For example, as your family meets people at church, there may be older adults or single young adults far from family with whom you find an affinity. These persons may become "special family friends" whom you invite to family holiday meals and birthdays or other special events. That incorporation may be a part of your mission statement, but that partnership may well change your mission statement too.

One more thing needs to be said about the mission statement and its importance for families and groups of individuals. As Christians, unless we know ourselves as disciples in mission, we have subverted our calling from God. If we use spiritual disciplines only to assure ourselves of a better life now or hereafter, we will not grow in faith. Rather, our participation in mission will not allow us to focus solely on ourselves or our small family unit. When we are in mission for others, whether the others are a block or a continent away, we find

ourselves facing God, perhaps not face to face, but heart to heart.

People throughout the centuries have acted on their calling from God and made dramatic changes in their lives. Francis of Assisi is well known for giving away his riches, even his clothes, to help the poor, much to the dismay of his father. Perhaps less well known is the story of Millard Fuller, the founder of Habitat for Humanity. Fuller, a successful lawyer, and his wife Sarah struggled with how to find more meaning in their life. This led them to Koinonia farm, where they worked with Clarence Jordan. They too gave their money to the poor and have worked ever since to help poor people own adequate and safe housing. However, dramatic change is not the only way we answer God's call. A family, after looking over the several mission programs of its congregation, might decide to include a shopping trip each month for the food pantry or to participate in the after-school program by all volunteering on a regular basis. Finally, only you, looking at the whole of your life, can make that determination with God's help.

Writing Your Mission Statement

1. Spend time in prayer with your family or those persons who are family to you. Seek God's will for your lives, not only separately, but together.

2. Meditate on Micah 6:6–8. How might you "do justice, love

mercy, and walk humbly with God" each day? How might you do that together? Many people think of stewardship or social action when they ponder these questions.

3. List on paper all the ideas that have come to each person. Post the page, make copies if necessary, where everyone will see it and have time to ponder it for a few days. Don't rush this process.

4. Together select the ideas that seem to be most important to your family or group of partners. Perhaps several ideas can be combined. Perhaps one idea prompted more thinking by other members and has now gained new importance. If you are facing a dramatic change in family life, invite one or two persons or another family you respect to help you find your way through this step. In the Quaker tradition, a meeting of this sort is known as a "clearness meeting." The guests ask open-ended questions rather than give advice. Their role is to keep you looking at all the possibilities until you are beginning to see your way clear to a decision. Such persons may open up avenues that you had not considered possible or point out alternatives that you have not explored.

5. Now write a mission statement of one paragraph. This should list two or three things that you will do together as your ministry in God's world, outside your family or group of friends. You may want to alter or totally rewrite your mission statement six months from now, so don't make it a burdensome task.

6. Print the mission statement in handsome letters or set it in an attractive font and print it on the computer. Post it where you can read it together at least once a week. Plan that time now so you don't forget.

7. Finally, pray and work at your mission statement. Intentionally set forth to fulfill the mission you have identified.

Summary

Called to live faithfully, our task is to discern how to do that in this place and time. Discovering that call and what it means is best ascertained with others, whether they be family or friends. In order to remember our call and the mission to which we are called, preparing a mission statement is essential. Throughout this process and throughout the living of our mission statement, we know that we can look to God in prayer and to Christ as a model.

Exercise: Spiritual Discipline

During a time when you are seeking to gain balance, you also need to maintain a strong connection with God. One way to do this is through the breath prayer, a simple prayer that can calm you as it reconnects you with your Creator.

A breath prayer is said as you breathe in and breathe out. It is repeated over and over. Its repetition allows you to center on your relationship with God and to be more open to receiving God's Spirit, the Holy Comforter. Say your breath prayer when you are rushing to work and must stop at a traffic light. Say it at home as you perform some chore with repetitious motions or a task that is done daily. Say it when you feel anger boiling up in you and there is no way to release it safely. Say it when you are lonely or happy. Pray your breath prayer anytime you want to be in touch with God. A wonderful thing about a breath prayer is that you can pray it anywhere, anytime, and no one else need know that you are praying. Just breathe deeply and pray your prayer silently.

Good phrases for breath prayers are:

—Come,/ Holy Spirit.
—Be with/ me, God.
—God's love/ is endless.

These prayers are marked to show the words you say silently as you inhale and those you say silently when you exhale.

Chapter Two
Not Enough Time, Too Many Choices

Jane and Carlos Williams reflected on their lives and their recent decisions and determined the convictions that were most important to them. They also talked about the role their faith plays in their life and affirmed their commitment to the church. Then they, along with their children, wrote a family mission statement. Now they are looking for ways to live according to it. They have found that each family member has different ideas about how they might do that together. Besides that, each family member has differing amounts of time, energy, and ability to devote to the activity they choose. Time seems to be at a premium; even time to talk about the selection seems to be hard to find. How, they wonder, will we ever get beyond this point?

❖—❖—❖—❖—❖

Martha and Esther helped Jennie discern some of the things important to her as she approaches retirement. In contrast to her friends' busy lives,

Jennie is anticipating more time at her disposal. However, she wonders how she will make choices as others request that time of her. She is grateful to her friends for their help and knows they will support her as she seeks to ascertain her gifts and how they might be used in the months ahead. However, this month as they have dinner together, Esther reports that she has received a promotion in her job. This job change will require some travel, and she is concerned about the increased frailty of her mother, who lives in another state. Martha notes, as they leave, that new kinds of decisions are facing her friends. As their individual lives change, they find their friendship and the assurance of their prayers for one another ever more important.

Time and choices are two common ingredients of nearly any decision about living faithfully. Who doesn't bemoan having too little time? Even Jennie may discover that there is not enough time to do all she wants to do when she retires. Yet every decision about time involves choices, sometimes more choices than any one person or family can handle. And when the time, choices, and other elements to take into consideration do not balance, still more choices are sought.

Let's begin with time. At least it is not infinite. One way to begin an examination of time is to read Ecclesiastes 3:1–15 as a meditation. Read it slowly, perhaps out loud, permitting your mind to wander and connect the words with specific events or stages in your life. You can do this alone or with others. If alone, write some of what comes to mind on paper or in a journal. With others, talk about what you remembered. This conversation can be particularly fruitful for a family group, as the various interpretations of important events are described.

Ecclesiastes 3:1–15

Ecclesiastes is one of the wisdom books of the Hebrew Scriptures. Unlike other biblical literature, it begins with the human situation and seeks God's revelation through it. These words of "the Teacher" (see 1:1) present a kind of early common sense at first reading. Each pair provides a balance, a biblical yin and yang. However, these verses are not as simple as first perceived or often portrayed. Some of the pairs include a time that is not what we want, such as "a time to kill," "a time to refrain from embracing," "a time to hate," or "a time for war."

The opposites named in the season and time for every matter are followed by a description of the task given us by God in verses 9–15. One message that can be drawn from this passage is that you must discern what season of God's time this is for you. Later, you may find that you are in a different time, but what is the task that God is giving you today?

As Christians, we also read Ecclesiastes in light of the death and resurrection of Jesus Christ. In Paul's second letter to the church in Corinth, we are reminded that all that we are and do is from God. Indeed, we strive to live "so that the life of Jesus may also be made visible in our bodies" (2 Cor. 4:10). Read 2 Corinthians 4:7–10, then read Ecclesiastes 3:1–15 again. Knowing that God through Christ Jesus is always within and with us, we can read even the more difficult seasons with the joy of that assurance.

God's Time

Another word needs to be said about time, specifically God's time. The Greek word *kairos* signifies a time that is set apart from the calendar time that generally demarcates our days and lives. Our life is so ruled by the twenty-four-hour blocks we call days that we can hardly imagine time in any other way. *Kairos,* however, is that special moment when God's call to us matches our time for action. Queen Esther lived in a moment of *kairos.* Mordecai reminded her of this when he said, "Who knows? Perhaps you have come to royal dignity for just such a time as this" (Esther 4:14).

We do not live daily in *kairos,* but we need always to be alert to the possibility. The moment of *kairos* may be in the midst of great difficulty or extreme uncertainty. This moment, as you reflect on your mission statement, may present a call from God that moves you into *kairos.* You may not recognize it as such until you have moved through it and can look back on the experience. Yet, no matter how you match your time and God's moment of *kairos,* you can be assured that God is with you even as you pray, "Come, Lord Jesus."

A Contemporary Time for Rest

A pairing of times that contemporary culture needs very much is not included in the list in Ecclesiastes 3:1–8: a time to work and a time to rest. Perhaps this is omitted because the time of rest, the Sabbath, that day when all refrained from work, was so much a part of the life of Israel. "Remember the sabbath day to keep it holy. Six days you shall labor and do all your work. But the seventh day is a sabbath to the LORD your God; you shall not do any work" (Exod. 20:8–10a).

More about a contemporary understanding of Sabbath time is found in the next chapter, but think about it for a moment now. When in your week, if ever, do you declare Sabbath time? Work or school schedules may dictate that you arrange your Sabbath time differently than it has been set up traditionally. Nevertheless, when do you join with others to acknowledge God's presence, and when do you extricate yourself from the demands of your work or others' requests so that you are able to live your mission statement as fully as possible? Tilden Edwards argues that arranging such a time in one's life brings its own teaching power. Living with this rhythm of ordinary time and Sabbath time teaches us what our calling is even as we live out that calling. Although a generous amount of Sabbath time is usually necessary for it to be effective, starting with two or three hours weekly can set the precedent. This humble beginning may lead you to something far greater than you now expect. Again, from Edwards: "A rhythm of sabbath and ministry time is a foundational discipline, a framework for all our disciplines. It is a rhythm that God provides to human life for its care, cleansing, and opening to grace. This rhythm is not for one day or one week or one year only. It is for life."[1] Through all this we can say with the psalmist, "But I trust in you, O LORD; I say, 'You are my God.' My times are in your hand" (Ps. 31:14–15).

Time and Choices

Before moving much further, you probably need to know where, in fact, your time does go. Whose demands are attended to first? Which blocks of time are negotiable and which are not? What rhythm has naturally developed in your allotment of time? What would you do with more time at your disposal?

The last question, of course, makes no sense. Time is finite. We, as a civilization, have made decisions about the division of time into minutes, days, weeks, years, centuries, but that does not increase the amount of time available to us. As much as we might like to find more time, we rarely can do that except as we discover shortcuts in our work or make decisions that allow us to use our time differently.

So we are back to choices and decisions. In order to see the choices before you, you need to know what decisions you are already working under. How is your time used now? Please pause now and, using copies of the form on page 79 as a guide, with

one page for each day, reconstruct the past week. Don't labor over what you cannot recall; try to identify the major blocks of time and how they were used. Then, beginning today, keep track of your time in thirty-minute blocks using the same form. Keeping this record will also help you in the spiritual discipline *examen,* described on pages 22–23. You will need at least a week's record to see the pattern created by your use of time. Each family member who can keep such a record should do so:

You may want to continue this record for a month to gain a more accurate picture of the days and rhythms you live. From time to time, check your calendar. How do seasonal changes or changes in your life affect these statistics? For example, the average week in the summer may be quite different from one in January, especially if you have school-age children or your work is influenced by the seasons of the year. A family change such as a major illness will also bring dramatic adjustments in the daily activities of those responsible for the person's care.

When you have compiled this record, try to look at it as though it is new material. What convictions does it exhibit by the amount of time allotted to each major activity, such as work, friends, family, education, or church? How do these allotments fit with the convictions you declared earlier? How do they fit with your mission statement? Rather than judging yourself, see this as a time of gathering information.

Next comes a harder task. Assume that nothing on your week's record is set in stone—not when you arrive at work, nor when you do the grocery shopping, nor when you sleep. If you lived each day according to your convictions and mission statement, what would your life look like during that "ideal" week? You may find this easier if you talk together first in general terms rather than specifics. Once you have sketched out such a week, you are ready to compare your ideal week with the actual week you recorded. What can you change about your actual week that will bring it closer to the ideal week? How can your week become more balanced so that it exhibits more clearly the convictions you want to convey? Where is the rhythm that will help you build and maintain your relationship with God?

Take this opportunity to arrange your week through wise and faithful choices rather than living by a "to do" list. Too often a list is worked through one item at a time, but little thought is given to evaluating the importance of the items in relationship to one another. Once you have a better sense of how you want to adjust the ways you use time, you may find within yourself a stronger resolve and a reason to say no to those requests that will not move you in the direction you have chosen. Here are some questions that you can use in this evaluation:

—Looking only at the size of the blocks related to any area, what appears to be most important in your life?
—What factors determine your use of time? Examples include the ages of your children, your work life, the health of family mem-

bers, household responsibilities, church responsibilities.
—During which blocks of time do you receive energy?
—During which blocks of time do you tire easily?
—Which blocks of time are the most flexible?
—(Write your own questions.)

As the Williamses struggled with matching their convictions and mission statement to their daily life, they first created a pie chart that showed the family time allotted to each major activity. As they discussed how the pie chart might look, other questions came to the fore: Why does one person carry the major responsibilities for the housework? How will decisions about the use of family together time be made? They decided how much time each week would be relegated to family time, which included evening meals, Sunday morning and much of the afternoon, and another evening at least once a month. Then they created a pie chart for how they wanted to allot their family time. (See the diagram below.)

After the first week or two, they discovered that there were times when only one parent and child could be engaged in their selected mission project. They decided to try dividing the responsibilities related to it. They also committed themselves to setting aside a time weekly that they would talk together about this participation. So, a further adjustment was made to their pie chart. They also found that they had to make concessions for the age, abilities, and needs of each child. They posted their pie chart and plan next to their mission statement.

On the other hand, Jennie, Martha, and Esther found that working together made it possible for them to participate more fully in their chosen mission projects. Together, Jennie and Martha could cover the mission project for Esther when she had to travel. Because this was a group commitment, they looked for ways the group could handle the commitment rather than parceling out equal hours and responsibilities to each woman.

As you already know, scheduling a life today that has any amount of interdependence with others is complicated. In working a plan like this, the help comes through the discussions about priorities and goals. While these will change over time, beginning with a base that everyone has helped develop will make the changes much easier to manage.

Discovering the Many Choices

Earlier it was noted that we have more choices about what we do and when we do it than previous generations had. Such a statement is always open to question, of course. Economic factors and other differences make this kind of statement true for some and not for others. The options before us may be altered by our economic sta-

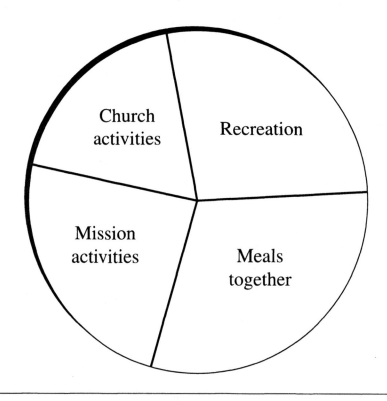

tus, culture or race, health, education, and many more factors. However, in our privileged North American culture, we do enjoy a wider variety of choices—about where we will live, go to school, vacation, eat lunch, as well as what we wear to work, listen to on the radio, and so on—than much of our world. Our wealth has brought us a multitude of choices; some provide us wonderful opportunity to spread God's love, while others are thrust upon us and are not of our choosing.

In spite of all these choices, or perhaps because of them, we may overlook more creative possibilities when it comes to examining how we live and how we want to live. Whatever the choices in your life, searching through those choices as well as creating a wider range of choices can be helpful only as you look for a way to simplify your life or live your faith more fully.

As you begin to think about changing to live according to your mission statement, an awareness of the choices you have is important. One method that can spark your imagination is to write a couple ideas for change related to your mission statement on separate sheets of paper. Then write as many choices as you can imagine for yourself on separate index cards. Don't dismiss any choices at this point, especially ones that you think are not realistic. Then play with the cards: alphabetize them, sort them by any categories you can design, stack them in order of difficulty or preference, draw two cards and try to combine them into one idea. As you work with the cards, add other ideas on more index cards. Leave the cards scattered on a surface or taped to a wall for a day or two, clustered around the potential change. You are not yet to a decision-making point.

The Good Enough Parent (or Child)

Our convictions and our reality often collide, particularly when we hold high expectations of ourselves as parents, as children caring for parents, or as spouses caring for spouses. We judge our success in these roles by how much we are able to do for the other person, often trying to meet impossible standards. For example, Esther, the only daughter in her family, may believe that her mother's care is finally up to her, even though her brother lives in the same town as their mother. Although women, especially daughters, are still the primary caregivers of parents, it is only reasonable that Esther's brother give a hand with her care. Similarly, in the Williams family with two fully employed parents, the household tasks need to be parceled out in terms of the availability of the individuals (children included!) and when they need to be done. Again, although many working women carry the larger load of household responsibilities, the Williams family need not follow that pattern.

If, when examining your week and what you would like it to be, you discover some expectations that may be unrealistic, ask yourself why you have these expectations. Did you inherit them from your family? Are they realistic expectations in today's world? In another era, Esther might have been expected to leave her job and go to live with her mother. Or Jane Williams and her daughter Maria might have been left with all the housework to do, even though Jane holds down a full-time job. What in your role as parent or caregiver is good enough and what can be set aside as unnecessary? Where we might once have thought that "we could have it all," most of us will clearly not have it that way all the time. More importantly, what of that "all" is most important to you? What matches your convictions? The Williamses can look for ways to share household responsibilities, to eliminate some that are found to be unnecessary, or even to barter some tasks, trading them with other families. Households in a congregation can also help one another. For example, someone can coordinate visitors to stay with a member who has dementia so that person's spouse is able to continue to use her or his gifts as a volunteer in ministry. Here is where a multitude of choices makes real sense; but we need to search for the less obvious choices.

Once you have begun to see some changes in your attitude and expectations, you will need to communicate these changes to others. This is particularly important if the expectations are held by the persons affected by the change. If Esther's brother assumes that Esther will be the primary caregiver for their mother because their mother cared for their grandmother, Esther will have to talk plainly with him about this matter. If Carlos Williams sees no reason for him or his

son to pitch in with cleaning the house on the weekend, Jane Williams will have to initiate that conversation and suggest ways that everyone can help clean the house they share. Even if parents agree, they will probably have to motivate their children to help. Such conversations are never easy, although they are sometimes not as difficult as anticipated. Ways to approach such conversations through improved communication skills are included in the next chapter.

Summary

Nearly every decision we make about our convictions and how we will live them involves the allocation of time and the selection among a variety of choices. Time is finite, but we can decide how we will use the time we have. In contemporary lives, the choices before us abound and grow more diverse and varied day by day. Some choices are helpful; others are hidden; and still others are thrust upon us. Therefore, we do ourselves a service by knowing how we already use our time. Then we can look at the choices before us and determine which choices will help us live the life to which God has called us.

Exercise: Spiritual Discipline

Examen is a daily practice of self-examination and prayer. Commonly done at the close of the day, it is a way to go back through your day and offer to God both the positive and negative events and emotions you experienced. While it can be done alone, conducting this spiritual discipline with your family or a friend can help you discover insights you might overlook on your own. In its simplest form, the *examen* follows these steps:

1. In your mind, go over the day. For what from the day are you grateful to God? Of those moments, which one would you choose as the key time? If with a person or group, name that time aloud.

2. Then, go over the day again. What from the day are you not grateful for or do you wish had not happened? Which moment caused you the most pain, either then or now as you recall it? If with a person or group, name that time aloud.

3. Pray to God for forgiveness for your role in that time for which you are least grateful. Also pray for any others involved in it and for their forgiveness.

4. Finally, recall that key time of the grateful moments. Pray, giving God thanks for that moment. Try to keep that moment in your heart as you go to sleep.

From time to time, invite family members or friends to name any directions or trends observed in the moments for which you are both grateful and not grateful over some weeks. Keeping a written record of your responses may help you detect patterns and trends on your own.

Many variations are possible when using the *examen.* Individual family members might agree to do this daily on their own and gather once each week to practice the *examen* together, using the week as the time frame for examination. A similar process might be instituted by a group of friends, who gather once or twice a month to use the *examen* together. Or a special church season, such as Advent, Christmastide, or Lent, can be the occasion that prompts a communal use of the *examen.*

In light of the topic of this book, the *examen* can be altered to include a focus on the family or group mission statement on a weekly, biweekly, or monthly basis. Along with looking for moments for which you are grateful or least grateful, recall moments when you were living the mission statement and times when you seemed to have forgotten it. One caution: center your thoughts and ideas on reflection of the group as a whole rather than judgment of individuals. Seek to determine how you are working as a unit, not how each one is living the mission statement. In this way, the focus is on being a working unit, living faithfully together, rather than on the perceived inadequacies of one member. In this way, each person can add to the group her or his special talents and be appreciated and accepted for that contribution. Judging is the responsibility of the individual conscience; judging comments from others are welcome only upon request, if at all.

Chapter Three
Moving Ahead

The Williams family struggled with selecting a way to improve their family life and the practice of their faith according to this mission statement: "We will practice Christian hospitality as a family." They considered many possibilities, from volunteering at a soup kitchen in a nearby city to offering to be greeters at their church on Sunday mornings. Finally, they decided to invite two or three older church members to their home for a meal after church one Sunday each month. A few months before,

Jane Williams learned about "Sabbath time" in a prayer group she attends, and she has been thinking about it ever since. This discussion seemed the right time to tell her family what she was thinking. While this plan is a small beginning at creating some Sabbath time for the family, every family member is comfortable with this plan and looking forward to their first guests.

❖⬥❖⬥❖⬥❖

Jennie, Martha, and Esther have begun to focus on the changes in

Esther's life. The three women have had several conversations about ways to adjust their commitment to helping others so that Esther's new responsibilities at work and for her mother can be honored. Jennie has offered to help entertain Esther's mother when she comes for a visit in a few weeks. Both Martha and Esther, however, struggle daily with bringing the various strands of their lives together in a tension that is creative rather than stifling.

Matthew 13:1–9, 18–23

Read the parable of the seed in Matthew 13:1–9 and 18–23. As you read this parable, focus on the seeds that are cast rather than on the sower. What permits the seed to grow?

In his commentary on the Gospel of Matthew, Douglas Hare provides a fresh interpretation of this parable for us:

> The general tenor of the message [in Matt. 13:1–23] is clear: those who receive the word of the kingdom and *understand* it, that is, appropriate it not merely intellectually but with a commitment at the depths of their being, will be able to withstand the onslaught of temptation and tribulation and produce a bountiful harvest in terms of the good fruits of obedience to God's will. . . . The commitment of today's Christians is threatened less by persecution than by secular scorn ('You don't really believe all that stuff, do you?'), but otherwise little has changed [since Matthew interpreted this parable for his church and culture]. The cares of the world and the deceitfulness of riches are still able to choke the word. Christians must pray for the gift of understanding, so that what they believe with their minds may be acted out in their daily behavior.[1]

From Statement to Action

Think of your mission statement as the seed. What might keep it from growing or sprouting into life? What would choke it back when you think you are ready to act on it? What could trample it down when you have made the first move, large or small? Now, how can you protect it and nourish it so that it can grow upright and strong? Take a few moments to ponder what you and the others in your family or group need in order to bring forth fruit from your mission statement. Don't settle for the first idea that pops into your mind. Include even those ideas that do not seem feasible at this point. Then ask yourself, Who might help in feeding and growing this mission statement?

A mission statement is nothing more than a dream if you are not actively working to make it part of your life. Read yours again. Recall the conversations based on the previous chapter. If you lived by your mission statement, what would your life be like? What would each day be like? When the Williams family tried this, they realized that little about Sunday set it apart as a day to worship God, and that Sunday morning activities felt unconnected to the rest of their week. The hour or so they spent at church was lost in the activities of the rest of the day. When Jane Williams told the family about Sabbath time and the book she had read, they agreed that it was a concept worth working on. From this and their mission statement they devised the plan to invite older people for lunch one Sunday a month.

Use your mission statement as a vision for your life. Look through your week for small steps that move you toward that vision. The ideas you came up with in the previous chapter are the starting blocks for this step in the process. Perhaps you see the need to build a closer relationship with God, and decide to spend five minutes in prayer before you get out of bed or before the rest of the family arises. Or you might decide that volunteering at the food pantry once a month would move you closer to your vision.

Selecting an area may not happen for you or your family quickly. You are on no strict timetable. Let the ideas work on you as you go about your week. Check in periodically with the family, or take a few moments to ponder where your subconscious thoughts have taken you. If you are doing this on your own, talk with a trusted friend as you seek to discern your path. Your decision may well come through a persistent alertness to see where God is leading you.

Keep in the open the host of choices about the change you wish to make. This will be easier if you wrote them on index cards or slips of paper as suggested in chapter 2. Ponder the possibilities as you wait for the coffee to finish brewing or watch for your car-pool ride. Jot notes next to them as new thoughts come.

The time will come, however, when you must make a decision about a step to take. Remove all the potential actions or choices that are not feasible, whether because the timing is wrong or because you simply do not find them challenging or interesting. Then, have each family member, one at a time, remove one choice. However, before it is thrown out, there must be a consensus for this action by the family. When the choices have been narrowed to three or four possibilities, stop and pray. Pray that you will be guided to a choice that is worthy of God's love. Then talk together until you come to an agreement. When that happens, pray again, inviting each person to offer a brief prayer of thanksgiving or request for God's help. Post your choice where you will all see it often. Now begin to plan how you will live with your choice and live it out.

Selecting a choice for change

1. Write all the choices you can imagine on index cards.

2. Post them where you can read them often.

3. After several days, remove the suggestions that are not feasible.

4. Come to agreement about other choices to eliminate.

5. Pray for God's guidance as you continue.

6. Together select one suggestion to try.

7. Pray for God's help as you live this change.

Moving Ahead or Pulling Back

As you have looked over how you use your time and the choices before you, you may have discovered that moving ahead means pulling back or turning away from something. Look through your week. What could be eliminated and barely missed? What might be eliminated for a time, because of other priorities in your life at this moment? Think back to the "shoulds" that you grew up with. Which ones are still ruling your life? Which ones are still necessary? Which ones help or inhibit living your mission statement?

Sabbath Time

The term "Sabbath time" we alluded to earlier comes from the Sabbath observed by the people of God as far back as the exodus. The Israelites rested on the seventh day, the Sabbath, emulating God's rest after creation. They refrained from any unnecessary work and gathered to praise God and give thanks. Many laws about the observance of this day can be found in the Hebrew Scriptures, especially Deuteronomy. The Pharisees chastised Jesus for allowing his followers to pick grain on the Sabbath (Matt. 12:1–8). Some people rebuked Jesus for healing on the Sabbath (Luke 13:10–17).

In the past, many states created laws that forbade doing business on the Christian Sabbath, Sunday. These "blue laws" have all but disappeared in North America, but the idea of a Sabbath need not be tossed out with them. When there was a common day of rest throughout a community, it was easier to observe a Sabbath. Certainly people had fewer choices about what to do, and even those options were likely not to interfere with Sunday morning worship. In our multifaith and multiculture society, some Christians must work on Sunday, and other events draw us from worshiping God with our faith community. However, observing the Sabbath, whenever that is possible for us during each week, can be an important spiritual discipline, helping us to deepen our relationship with God and with our Christian community.

Tilden Edwards suggests these simple steps in developing a Sabbath time appropriate to our unique situation:

—Pray, over a span of days, for God's direction as to the rightness of this practice for you.
—Talk about this concept with other family members or those who can support you in the practice.
—Begin your preparation on Saturday by doing what chores you can that you would ordinarily do on Sunday. Have a special meal on Saturday night as a way of readying yourself for the Sunday Sabbath. Use rituals of prayer and candlelighting to set this time apart.
—On Sunday morning, have a time of silent prayer. Read the lectionary passages, especially if your pastor preaches from the lectionary (a schedule of Bible readings for worship so that most of the Bible is covered over a three-year period). Prepare for worshiping with your congregation.

—Plan a way to conclude the Sabbath, marking the end of it with prayer, candlelighting, or other rituals that will help you bring this time to an end.[2]

The key to developing a Sabbath time is finding the rhythm of your life and placing the Sabbath where it fits naturally. Esther may decide that she wants to visit her mother one weekend a month. Therefore, the time that she, Jennie, and Martha come together for their Sabbath time may be altered on those weekends. Or they may find that another time during the week works better for all of them. In examining your life for the place for Sabbath time, take account of the stage of your life, the culture in which you live, the configuration of your family or friendship group, and the rhythm established by your work, school, and family responsibilities.

Finally, do so with humor and joy. Finding and celebrating Sabbath time should help you enter into a relationship with God and one another that adds joy to your life. As Delia Halverson notes in *Living Simple, Simply Living,* "Happiness happens on the outside. Joy dwells deep within. Joy is not a goal but a by-product of service."[3] As you establish a Sabbath time related to your mission statement, keep alert to when you experience joy. Build on such times.

The Ripple Effect of Change

When you have chosen your first step, imagine that action. Who around you will be affected by it? Any change in your life, however small or seemingly inconsequential, creates a ripple. Those persons closest to you are hit by the ripple first, but others whose lives touch yours are also affected. In a family, you might ask each member to describe how this change will affect her or him. Then talk together about how others will be affected, particularly persons with whom you have significant contact, such as employees or employers, close friends, teachers, extended family members, neighbors, or church members.

When you toss this small pebble—the change you have selected—into your life, who will feel the ripples? These persons can either help you with the change, or they can resist the effect the change has on them, making the change more difficult for you. Look at the list of persons you have made. How can you prepare them for the ripple that will reach them?

Developing Better Communication Skills

Whatever the necessary message, good communication skills are critical. To that end, here are some exercises to help you evaluate how you communicate and improve your communication skills.

First, how do you communicate with family members or within your family or circle of close friends? In *Family the Forming Center,* Marjorie Thompson writes: "To love in God's way involves generous self-giving. A vital family life requires a great deal of give and take—capacity for compromise, yielding to others, and graciously being yielded to. We will find it hard to give ourselves freely to others when we are judging them. . . . The condemning face of judgment is a form of withholding personal acceptance, thus a way of withholding the self."[4] The manner in which we speak to another person may speak more loudly than our words, particularly if the manner and the words do not convey the same message. Take time to evaluate how you communicate (and listen) before you seek to deliver your message.

Whether you are a spouse, a parent, or a single adult, you are likely to find yourself describing this change to a family member or close friend, one from whom you seek encouragement and support. You may also seek the support of an employer or someone in your career arena. Two hints for how you frame what you say:

—Speak positively. Rather than focusing on the difficulty you might anticipate, highlight the beneficial aspects of this change for you and others.
—Avoid language that judges the listener. In explaining your choice and plan, try not to imply that other choices are less than right or faithful or good.

Three basic components make up any moment of communication: the speaker, the listener, and the message. Effective communication occurs when a message sent in words or writing by one person is the same as that received by another person. Your inflection and body posture help the receiver understand your message.

Have you ever written a letter that was misinterpreted? If you had spoken the words, your inflection and tone of voice might have provided the necessary ingredients so that the message would have been interpreted as you intended. Only about 7 percent of what we communicate is conveyed by our words; another 38 percent by our tone of voice; and 55 percent by our body language. For clarity in communication, all three aspects of the message must be congruent.

Say this sentence: "I'm glad you're finally home." How many ways can you interpret it by varying your tone, body language, or word emphasis? How would you say it to a teenager who comes home after curfew? To a child who has been missing for several hours? How might a mother of three preschool children say the sentence when her husband walks in from work? Or how might a child who had received an honor at school that day say it?

In an ongoing conversation, we play the roles of both speaker and listener. Therefore, when we wish to communicate an important idea, we have to be prepared to listen so we can continue to interpret our message. Again, a word from Marjorie Thompson, "Often we find ourselves distracted or preoccupied by tasks, problems, feelings, and fantasies. . . . It takes effort and intention to focus on the presence of another person, as well as a willingness to give oneself over to the need of the other at a given time. Such presence is the root of authentic listening, and listening is the foundation of real communication and communion among persons."[5]

When we have something important to communicate, we may be so intent on speaking our words that we fail to listen carefully to the other person's questions or comments. We may also be so sure of the rightness of our message that we cannot hear any questioning comments from the other person. A good exercise and method to help you focus on what the other person is saying is to repeat what the person said in your own words. This kind of listening is called *active listening.* Instead of being so concerned about what we are going to say next, which may have no bearing on what our communication partner has just said, we must listen carefully to the other person. Then we can take time to incorporate that message into our thoughts before we speak. This also allows the other person an opportunity to correct any misconceptions, which might make it impossible for us to communicate our message.

—Recall a recent conversation. Did it match these sentences about active listening?

—Active listening allows the other person to clarify his or her message by speaking directly to the specific misunderstanding you have revealed.

—Active listening demonstrates that you want to understand what the other person is saying.

—Active listening conveys interest in and respect for the other person.

—Active listening increases the accuracy of communication and degree of mutual understanding.

Try this in a conversation today. After a family member or friend speaks to you, giving a message that has content more than greeting, rephrase what you heard. You might begin with something like, "Do you mean . . . ?" or "Are you saying . . . ?" Not every sentence spoken to us requires rephrasing, of course, but using this method carefully will increase your listening ability and improve your communication. Bonnie Michaels uses this list of ten points for good listening[6] in her workshops on managing work and family:

1. Stop talking.

2. Put the speaker at ease.

3. Show the speaker you want to listen.

4. Remove distractions.

5. Empathize with the speaker.

6. Be patient.

7. Hold your temper.

8. Go easy on argument and criticism.

9. Ask questions.

10. Stop talking!

Now look again at the list of persons who will be affected by your change. How will you approach each one to describe your plan? What information does each one need? What do you need from each one to make this change?

Not only is communication important for letting others know of an impending change in your life that will affect them, but effective communication is important in the family or other circle of support. Unfortunately, too often the persons who get the short shrift in the communication pool are the persons who are most important to us. One way to open up the conversation that is stuck in superficial phrases is to avoid yes or no questions. Asking your spouse, "Did you have a good meeting?" may elicit a yes or no answer. However, asking, "What interesting thing happened at the meeting?" will prompt some thinking on the part of the spouse and open up an avenue of conversation for both of you.

A healthy communication model is present when one:

—listens
—doesn't interrupt
—compromises willingly
—expresses feelings
—accepts the feelings of others
—maintains an atmosphere of cooperation
—is willing to resolve conflicts
—is willing to talk through resentments

How do you rate your communication style?

Summary

In order to move ahead with the intent of the mission statement, you have several things to do. One is to determine one change that you can initiate immediately that will take you in the direction of the larger vision you have for your life of faith. To do so, you need to select it from among the widest choice you can imagine.

Once you have selected a change you want to make, think about how this change will affect others and the kinds of support and help you will need from these persons. To let others know about your planned change and to continue to talk about that change within your family or circle of friends, practice some improved communication patterns. Throughout this time, pray for God's support and guidance.

Exercise: Spiritual Discipline

Without prayer, we may not be able to determine the change that will move us closer to God's will. Without prayer, we will hardly be able to sustain our desired change. Without prayer, we may never discover the role of the other in our life of faith.

It is natural to seek God's help when we want to try something new or institute a change. Instinctively, we know that even the smallest change will not happen if we rely only on ourselves. Thus, we turn to God for help.

It is only natural to ask God to remove the obstacles from our path. We may ask God to help us convince others that their support and adaptation to our change is important, important enough to make their own changes. This, however, seems to go against the kind of active listening we have just discussed. Instead of telling God how the other persons need to support us or change for us, pray for the other person, leaving the plan up to God. You may be worried about the reaction of your employer or your aging parent to the change that you want to make. You may even feel antagonism toward the other person, whom you expect will try to block your change. Spend time in prayer for the person, seeking God's love and will for that person. When you have done this regularly, you may well find that your relationship with the person is slowly being transformed. Jesus told his disciples to love their enemies and pray for those who persecuted them (Matt. 5:44).

Chapter Four
Creative Problem Solving

The Williamses had entertained several older members of their congregation when they came upon Ethel Winter. When she and two other elderly women came for dinner, the conversation turned to grandchildren. Ethel was quiet. The Williamses knew that she had never married, but they were surprised to learn that she had been an only child. Now she had no living relatives at all.

Ethel still lived in the house where she had lived as a child. It was not a large house, but the lawn care alone was more than she could handle. As the family talked about Ethel during the week, they slowly came to the decision that they would include Ethel in more of their family activities and look for ways to give her a hand.

⎯⎯⎯✦⎯⎯✦⎯⎯✦⎯⎯✦⎯⎯✦⎯⎯

Jennie and Martha are finding themselves more and more caught up in Esther's dilemma and concern for her mother. It was clear that the care for her mother was taking increasing amounts of Esther's energy, even though her mother did not live nearby. Jennie heard about a support group for caregivers and suggested that they all attend. They did, and soon found that the conversations with others provided Esther (and her friends) the courage to face whatever came next.

At the same time these three friends continue to work on the other portion of their mission statement. They volunteer one Saturday morning a month at a local food pantry, where they bag groceries or do whatever needs to be done. This connection with another neighborhood in their community has opened their eyes to the inequities in the schools around them. When the director of the food pantry heard of Martha's background (she was an elementary school teacher for five years after college), he urged her to become involved in a campaign to improve the school in that neighborhood.

Mark 7:24–30

God is a God of surprises. Not even Jesus was immune to being surprised and changed by the unexpected. Read Mark 7:24–30, the story of Jesus and the Syrophoenician woman. This Gentile woman had a daughter possessed by a demon. That she is a Gentile is underscored in the text (v. 36), preparing us perhaps for what is to come. Still, as we read this story today, we are surprised, even shocked,

at the unfeeling response Jesus makes to her request. Is this the champion of all who are oppressed and broken-hearted, this man who implies that he has come for the Jews and that the Gentiles are the equivalent of dogs? He made no such harsh comment to the male foreigner with the demon he healed earlier (Mark 5:1–20). Is it because a woman is speaking to him? Whatever the reason, Jesus does answer her in this way. Just as surprising is the woman's response. Not only is her retort surprising, but she is the only person in the Gospel of Mark to corner Jesus, forcing him to reverse his decision. Where did she gather the courage to insist that she and her daughter deserved his attention? How could a woman speak so forthrightly in the presence of a stranger, particularly a man? Yet her words convince Jesus to heal her daughter.

On the one hand, the focus of this incident is on Jesus. Through it he displays God's wondrous glory, the glory that surprises us over and over. Through this single incident, Jesus expanded his mission to include all those who would approach him. This tiny moment, included also in the Gospel of Matthew, reminds us that God is the God of all creation and prepares us for the mission to the Gentiles given to Peter, followed by a mission to the world given to Paul.

Think about each person in this story. Begin with the woman. What was the surprise for her? How do you suppose she knew of Jesus and that he was in Tyre? Then think about the daughter, the child who was suddenly dispossessed of this difficulty. She was lying on the bed when her mother returned and found "the demon gone." We do not know her age. Perhaps she had lain unconscious for days or had thrashed about on the cot, tormented day and night. What was the surprise for her? And what about the people in whose home Jesus was staying? What was the surprise for them? Do you suppose they hinted, with a certain pride, that Jesus was their guest? Did they regularly entertain Gentiles, such as the woman? Finally, what about Jesus? What was his surprise? How might it have changed his ministry?

When has something unexpected happened to you, something that caused you to reevaluate some aspect of your life? Perhaps it was a request for help or an encounter with a stranger that brought a new perspective to the way you think about others. Look back over the last few weeks to see when God surprised you. The Williams family was surprised by Ethel Winter, and in that moment discovered a concentrated focus for their ministry. Who—young or old, friend or foe, neighbor or stranger—has broken into your insulated world and shaken your repose? What resulted from that moment, that tiny bit of God's time, of *kairos*?

Meeting the Unexpected

When Jennie suggested that she and Martha go with Esther to the caregivers' support group, she had no idea what to expect. She did not expect, however, that this would bring them into a new circle of loving care. The three women learned about the demands of caregiving, even caregiving at a distance. Little had they expected that their decision to work together on a mission statement would lead them to this place and time. As they talked about the group at their weekly dinner together, they began to recognize a shift in how they would live their mission statement. The change in Esther's responsibilities, family and work, was shifting the ground under each of them. The recognition that Esther's mother needed more help was affecting each of them in ways they had not anticipated.

What about your life? How has putting into motion the change that you selected affected your day-to-day activities? What surprises have you encountered? How have you changed?

One family, in an effort to be more careful of how they used the earth's resources, agreed that for any trip a mile or less from their home they would walk rather than drive the car. Having made the decision in the summer, the transition was relatively easy. But when fall and then winter arrived, their commitment was tested. Did the weather make a difference to their commitment? Would they still walk the distance after dark? Factors accompanying even the smallest change, from the safety of the neighborhood to the health of the family member involved, can alter the decision.

You have probably not been involved in your change long enough to experience many alterations in the significant factors surrounding it. However, variations in your family configuration, work responsibilities, church responsibilities, and stage of life will all make a difference in how that change works. You well know what a shift in all of one's life the arrival of a new family member makes, but the departure of a child for college makes a similar shift. The family above who decided to walk any place within a mile from their home can expect to experience a rift in that plan when their older child gets a driver's license. How will they handle the request for the car to pick up one or two friends before going to the choir rehearsal, when the church is less than a mile from their home? What other unrelated shifts might force them to reexamine this decision? Even though made for economic and environmental reasons (and good stewardship), the factors related to this decision—as well as virtually any decision—are not solely in the hands of the family or individual.

How will the Williams family make the adjustments required to include Ethel Winter in their holiday and special family activities? In their example, we easily see that a change is not forever. Having found that Ethel needs their friendship and help more than the other older adults they entertained, they will probably decide to concentrate on her, rather than inviting a different group of older adults to their home each month. You too will revisit your decision from time to time as circumstances require. Not only will your change create ripples in your

life, it may well ignite sparks that brighten all that you do together.

Some people, when obstacles or questions surface because of their desired change, throw up their hands, saying, "I knew this wouldn't work!" The Syrophonecian woman might have responded in this manner when Jesus spoke so brusquely to her. Fortunately for her daughter and ultimately for us, she did not. She was not stopped by tradition or cultural mores. Her example can give us courage as we seek our own solutions when lesser obstacles stop us.

Adapting to Meet New Obstacles

Recognizing that life is a series of changes helps us when we encounter unexpected ones. Parents quickly learn that just when they have adjusted to a particular stage of childhood, they are likely to see their child move to the next one. Caregivers of memory-impaired adults live through similar shifts, but in the opposite direction and with less hope. Sometimes we forget that adulthood is much the same way. While the stages may be more subtle, looking over our lives we can see that change is what life truly is all about. With change come new problems to solve or, put more positively, new opportunities for growth. Therefore, developing good problem-solving skills is to our advantage, even when we do not intend to institute a change.

Since we cannot predict what problems we will encounter, recognizing the steps in problem solving and being creative problem solvers will always stand us in good stead. Here are some hints about developing that stance:

—Look at the problem from a variety of angles. Just as you examined the story of the Syrophoenician woman from the viewpoint of each person in the story, looking at a problem from the point of view of every person involved can bring fresh insights. Especially helpful is taking the point of view of the person traditionally opposite you. So a parent might try to explain the problem from the point of view of a child or the child from the point of view of a grandparent. Here is where the listening skills you have developed will also be helpful.

—State the important questions related to the problem. The way you phrase a question or describe a problem can open it up for a variety of solutions, or it can shut off the possibility of solutions. In *The Fifth Discipline,* Peter Senge talks about the need to look beyond the personal. When we state the question in relation to our point of view, we will seek answers only from that point of view. More creative solutions may be found by stating the primary question in several ways. Both this method and the one above are akin to the parables that Jesus told. They turned the usual point of view upside down. Look for the questions that do that to your problem.

—Bring in others to stimulate your creativity. Noted in chapter 1 was the Quaker practice of the clearness meeting (page 13), where the person with the problem to solve or a decision to make calls together three or four friends for help. These friends do not provide answers, but they ask questions, probing each angle or possibility of the situation. Perhaps you did something like this as you chose the change you wanted to make.

—Look for the positives brought about by the change. When we encounter a difficulty, we may forget the positive aspects that the change has brought to our life. Even as you seek a way through this difficulty, celebrate the good that the change has brought to you.

—Be flexible. Be willing to adapt and adjust the decision you made about the change. There is a season for each action and work. Recall the words in Ecclesiastes 3. Have you come to a time of the opposite of what you began? Of course, flexibility may not mean a reversal of your decision. It may, however, suggest that as a family you need to consider how the change is affecting each family member. Or flexibility may indicate the helpfulness of taking another look at some detail of the way you choose to put your mission statement into action.

—Find support for your change. The caregivers' support group that Martha, Jennie, and Esther attended is one example of how meeting with others in a similar situation can be helpful. Look around your congregation for role models or mentors who can help you. Instituting change can be lonely, particularly when the change goes against the grain of the culture around you. While a strengthened spiritual life will sustain you, knowing that others stand with you provides additional power.

To problem-solve creatively

—Look at all the angles.
—State the key questions.
—Seek ideas from others.
—Look for the positive.
—Be flexible.
—Find support.

If you want to perk up your creative thinking, try this activity. Select any ordinary household item. The kitchen is a good place to look. Place it on the table. Then, alone or with others, discuss one of these questions: "How is my problem like this item?" "How might this item be used (actually or metaphorically) to resolve our problem?" Have fun with this activity. The creative juices flow more freely when we laugh and get a little silly.

Another approach to setting loose your creative thought is to ponder some of these questions:

—What is the obvious or "right" answer?
—What is the less obvious or next "right" answer?

—What kind of animal is this problem like?
—What do you feed that animal or problem to make it feel good?
—How would you solve this problem if it were upside down?
—What is the key word or phrase in the problem?
—How can you use that key word or phrase in restating the problem? In naming a solution?
—What metaphor or symbol is hidden in the problem statement?
—How might this metaphor be used to solve the problem? Think of at least three ways to do this.
—What spoken or unspoken rules are attached to this problem?
—Which rules are really necessary? Which ones can be tossed out?
—What "what if" questions can you ask about this problem?
—Consider each person affected by this problem. How would each one complete this sentence: The best thing to do about this problem is . . .
—If this problem were a cartoon, what would it be?
—What is the weirdest solution that you can think of for this problem?
—Go around the circle at least four times for everyone to complete this sentence: If I had this problem, I would . . .

Only when we have dreams and visions of the future, a future that is different from the present, are we alive to God's possibilities for us. The new life we have in Christ makes it possible for us to begin again and again, even beyond the seventy times seven. We need not despair when we falter along the way, for God continues with us. The obstacles encountered as you seek to live faithfully and to bring a creative, lively tension to your existence may alter the path you began, but these same obstacles may open your eyes and heart to new expressions of God's love and work in your life.

Delegating

Mothers who work outside the home are often the best models for the art of delegating. However, we all need to understand the importance of this skill if we are to live out our mission statements. We know that we need a strong relationship with God. Nevertheless, we sometimes expect that we can live our lives on our own. Nothing could be further from the truth.

Take Ann, for example. She agreed to teach a church school class. She is single, but has always enjoyed children and is looking forward to the time with this group. As she looks over the leader's guide, she sees a number of interesting activities. Some she knows she can lead; others she feels are beyond her experience. When she agreed to teaching, the church school superintendent assured Ann that other adults in the church were willing to lend a hand. As Ann thinks about involving them, she wonders if it isn't easier to do it herself than to ask others or try to coordinate their efforts. She also has a

nagging sense that she since she accepted this task, she should do it all. That, combined with a bit of guilt about asking others, especially parents working outside the home, has kept her from calling on others to share their gifts with the children.

How about you? Do you find it hard to ask for help, or even to invite others to join you in a task? Delegating is "the art of getting someone else to do it."[1] We can call on the strengths of others to complement our own, or we can ask for help because the task must be shared. Too often our image of the "perfect" parent, teacher, volunteer, or worker keeps us from delegating those parts of the job that can be done by others. As you look at your mission statement and how you want to accomplish it, you are surely going to have to find ways to delegate and share tasks. Here are some hints about delegating that work:

—Acknowledge that others can do the job. The fact that you are the parent or you agreed to a task does not mean that no one else can do it. While other people may not do it the way that you would, they can complete the task. Your assignment is to be clear about what is needed and to accept the job they do.

—Expect others to participate. Do not approach the person whose help you need with your hat in your hand and begin by apologizing for asking. Most people, children included, want to be helpful. Neither is it helpful to give all the reasons why you are asking. Say what you need, and assume they will say yes. Jesus called disciples, delegating his ministry among them.

—Communicate clear expectations. For a family task, break the task into smaller jobs so everyone can participate. Be specific about the role of each family member. When possible, however, allow the person to determine how to accomplish the task rather than demanding that it be done the way you would do it. Your communication skills will be put to the test here. Also be clear about the deadline for completion and the quality that is necessary.

—Say thank you. Give praise and thanks to those who accepted and completed tasks.

Delegation can contribute to including everyone in the family or circle of friends as you implement your mission statement. It may also be important as you rearrange your daily activities to make your desired change possible. Delegation, however, is a means to the goal, not the goal itself.

Summary

While we can often anticipate what will happen as a result of a change, we can never plan for everything that one change will bring to our lives. One strategy for dealing with the "sparks" that come is to problem-solve creatively. To do so, we need an openness to new possibilities and ideas, as well as a willingness to let go of what did not work for us. Another important

strategy is delegation. Opening up a task to the participation of others can be freeing for us as well as self-affirming for them.

Exercise: Spiritual Discipline

The Psalms of the Hebrew Scriptures are the hymnbook of the people of God. As such, they describe many emotions and the complexities of the people's relationship with God. Being familiar with only selected psalms and, too often, minute portions of them, many Christians are surprised at the depth and breadth of feelings displayed by the authors of this book in the Hebrew Scriptures.

Many people have found in the Psalms the words they could not speak on their own as they prayed to God. Important to us when we are up against a difficult problem is the knowledge that God is always with us. For that assurance, one place we can turn is to Psalm 107. If, however, we find ourselves besieged by those who are not supportive of our change, Psalm 142 may be more heartening for us.

Select a psalm. If it would be helpful, play soft music as you read. Read it slowly, reflectively. Allow the words to sink into your head and heart. When you come to a phrase or verse that particularly catches your attention, sit with it for a moment or two. Say it over and over aloud or silently. Read the psalm several times, allowing it to enter your head and become your prayer. Sit silently when you are ready, seeking God's word for you, listening with the depths of your soul.

If this type of praying is new to

you, start with only a few minutes of silence. Allow your body and mind to become accustomed to doing nothing. Some people find that repeating their breath prayer clears their mind for this type of prayer. Others find quiet instrumental music helpful to blot out other sounds. If your mind wanders to other concerns, call yourself back and try again. There is no need to batter yourself when this happens; it is a common occurrence, even for those with long experience in this type of prayer.

Listening for God takes practice. For some people, it comes easily. For others, it takes more preparation. For most people, the quiet time of meditation has a value of its own in our rushed world. Start small with just a few minutes, and slowly increase the time in this kind of prayer. You may find a period when listening for God yields nothing. Persons who have used this spiritual discipline for years

have times when it simply does not work, when prayer doesn't work. In an article about praying in difficult times, Roberta Bondi wrote: "Whatever might take place, however, I hope I can remember what I have learned—that prayer is a surprising gift that God sometimes gives to us in its most powerful form during the very times we are most tempted to think that we are failing."[2] Keep this thought in your heart.

Naturally, contemporary hymns can be used as prayers in the same way. Perhaps you have already found that a familiar hymn or part of one comes to you when you least expect it, a reminder of God's love and mercy. Some hymns that others have found helpful are "If You Will Only Let God Guide You," "Send Me, Jesus," and "Be Still, My Soul." Look through the hymnbook used by your congregation for hymn texts that can be your prayer in the future.

Chapter Five
Keep On Keeping On

The Williamses continued to include Ethel Winter in their family life. Ethel and Maria struck up a special friendship. They sat together at worship and Ethel delighted Maria with stories of her childhood. When school began, however, and the routines for each family member tightened, including Ethel was not so easy. All the rush of beginning school, choir rehearsals at church, sports practices after school—not to mention homework and household chores—kept everyone busy.

At a recent family meeting, thirteen-year-old Richard told of the youth group plans to rake leaves for senior citizens living in the church neighborhood. Suddenly he said, "I could do that for Ethel. She doesn't live in the church neighborhood, but I bet a couple of us could go over there and rake leaves."

At this point in the discussion, the family began to look more seriously at what they were able to do during the school year and what they thought Ethel needed. It was clear that she could benefit from more help than they were able to give right now. Jane Williams offered to call the church and talk with their associate pastor, who worked with the various volunteer groups in the church. They now knew Ethel well enough that they were sure she would not ask for help, but they could direct others to her.

⊲◇⊷◇⊷◇⊷◇⊷◇⊳

Fortunate to have the support of Jennie and Martha, Esther is finding ways to balance the new and changed aspects of her life. Nevertheless, she is always on the lookout for ways to relieve stress, particularly when elements beyond her control are pushing and tugging at her. For example, last Saturday her mother called twice to ask when Esther was coming to visit. Esther explained that she was planning to come in two weeks, but the way her mother accepted that information pulled at Esther's heartstrings.

Esther sat for a moment and prayed her breath prayer before she returned to getting ready to join Martha in the Saturday tutoring and mentoring program at the food pantry building. Martha had taken the children who needed help there to her heart. When she found that the library was not open on the weekend due to budget cuts, she asked about setting up a tutoring program in a nearby church. To begin this program, Martha had to pull out of the volunteer work

with her friends. After they discussed the situation together, they agreed that the need was great and that Martha had the gifts to do something about it. Martha is now thinking about asking her coworkers to volunteer one Saturday a month.

Colossians 3:9–17

Read Colossians 3:9–17. These verses begin with a reminder to the readers that they have done away with their old selves. The new self is based on Christ. After this reminder, Paul elaborates on what this new self is like. This new self is clothed in compassion, kindness, humility, meekness, patience, a willingness to forgive, and love. Once more, as in 1 Corinthians, love is the binder or adhesive that holds everything together in perfect harmony. Clothed in this manner, we work not for ourselves but in the name of Christ Jesus.

But wait a minute! "Perfect harmony." How can we possibly achieve perfect harmony? In his commentary on Colossians, Ralph P. Martin describes perfect harmony as "an integrative whole with no part out of place or lacking."[1] Isn't that what we mean by balancing our personal, work, and church responsibilities? Harmony is not the same as equality, giving each person or task the same amount of time or energy, no matter what. Nor is it giving up one's self to avoid discord until there is nothing left in you to give. Harmony in music is the selection of notes to be played or sung together to create a pleasing sound.

For our harmonic balance, we seek to select those tasks or responsibilities that when put together create a faithful life, a perfect harmony that brings us into harmony with all of God's creation. However, this harmony involves not just the parts that are all there, but the way that we use the attributes named by Paul to perform the tasks related to these parts. The notes in a piece of music change, or there would be no music. The "notes" in our lives change too, or there would be no growth. As the tasks in our lives change, however, the base on which we rest is not altered because all that we do, we do "in the name of the Lord Jesus, giving thanks to God the Father through him" (Col. 3:17).

In a small, or perhaps large, way you have been putting your old self behind and taking on a new self as you wrote a mission statement and set out to change some part of your life. You have sought to create a more perfect harmony within your life—individually and as a family or group of friends. The call to the Christians in Colossae and to each Christian today is to be more fully clothed in these virtues so that we might answer our call in the name of Jesus Christ. When Christ dwells within us, we speak with one another not only with wisdom, but with love. We give thanks for Christ to God, and our hearts are filled with songs of gratitude and joy.

When we feel discouraged, we would do well to return to these verses and ponder the new self within us. We will surely be discouraged and find ourselves caught up in the things that we wanted to leave behind. Discord or harmonic imbalance may set us on

edge. We may not be able to pray. For those times, we also need to know where we can find support for the changes we seek, the new life God calls us to, indeed the new life Christ promises us.

Finding Support

The smoothest change can hit a rocky road or even a roadblock. We know from the words of Paul and others that our relationship with God can strengthen us for the difficult times. Of course, we know from them that we will falter also. The spiritual disciplines described in this book (breath prayer, *examen,* intercessory prayer, praying the Psalms) are an important means of support.

Other disciplines build our spiritual muscles as well. The practice of hospitality, welcoming others to our home or workplace or church, can introduce us to the face of God in many guises. The practice of fasting, whether from food or excessive purchases, prompts us to examine our needs, especially those wants that separate us from God. The meditative reading of Scripture may open our eyes and mind to a fresh understanding of God's word for us. (For more on the use of spiritual practices, see the books in the bibliography.)

We also find support from other family members who have the same commitment. If you have practiced the self-giving defined by Marjorie Thompson earlier (see pages 28–29), you may have found that your family relationships are less marred by judgment and are built on the recognition that each person is a child of God, fully loved by God. Then, when you find yourselves in disagreement, you try to work it out rather than turn from the other person. Use your support for one another to keep the conversation going. Call forth the communication skills you learned as you began to change your lives. You will find that you are strengthened by your disagreement and better able to meet the questions and skepticism of those outside your family or your immediate circle of friends.

The Great Cloud of Witnesses

Along with the support we find in our relationships with God and family members, we can look beyond our family and ourselves to the world beyond. A first place to look for support is your congregation. Perhaps you have already identified persons who are interested in your desire to change. Perhaps you know of persons who have already found ways to live out the change you have chosen. Talk with these people. Seek their wisdom and prayers. Invite them to be your mentors. They will probably be eager to share what they have learned and more than happy to include you in their prayers.

The people you seek in your congregation are just the first step to discovering the great cloud of witnesses the writer of Hebrews describes (Heb. 11:2). We have already noted the support we can gain from reading the Bible meditatively, but we can also gain if we go to Scripture to learn of the struggles and successes of God's

people, people just like us. Read about Esther, David, Daniel, and Ruth in the Old Testament or Hebrew Scriptures. Meet the prophets, who surely had their share of adversity as they prodded the people toward change and renewal. Then turn to the New Testament and read about Peter, Paul, Dorcas, and the many unnamed Christians who populated the early church.

However, do not stop with the Bible. Read biographies of Christians through the centuries. Read about the martyrs of the early church and about Christians who have lived outside the dominant culture. Meet contemporary Christians who have answered God's call with dramatic change, such as Millard Fuller, Harriet Tubman, Albert Schweitzer, and Mother Teresa. Allow their strength to strengthen you.

Reading may be inspiring, but a heart-to-heart chat cannot be beat. Search for a friend who will listen and ponder your choices with you. Finding the right person may not be easy, but the search will be worth it. Look back at the description of the clearness meeting of the Quakers (page 13). Whom do you know with the gifts to help you examine your life lovingly?

Sometimes the stress related to change builds and builds. Nothing takes it away, and its high level keeps us from being our new self. You cannot live without some stress, but you can try to keep stress at a manageable level. Caregivers of older adults are constantly advised to take time for themselves. That advice is important for all of us. Try one of these stress relievers on a regular basis.

—Sit in a straight chair. Play soft music. Relax each part of your body, beginning with your toes and going to the top of your head. Do this two or three times. Give particular attention to the areas of your body that are tense.

—Exercise daily. Walk, jog, bike, or do whatever fits your interest or schedule.

—Do nothing for at least five minutes. Sit with your hands in your lap and your eyes closed. Take yourself to a place that rests you, all of you.

—Call a friend who usually makes you laugh. If your friend is not at home, read the comics in your newspaper.

—Breath deeply for several minutes.

—Get a back rub or a massage.

—Spend half an hour or so with a favorite hobby, one in which you can immerse your whole being.

—Read inspirational quotes that you have collected.

—Pray.

When the lawyer asked Jesus which commandment in the law was the greatest, Jesus answered, " 'You shall love the Lord your God with all your heart, and with all your soul, and with all your mind.' This is the greatest and first commandment. And a second is like it: 'You shall love your neighbor as yourself' " (Matt. 22:37–39). Unless we care for and love ourselves, we will not be able to love others and carry out our mission statements.

Summary

Finally, we return to the understanding that we, as children of God, do not operate alone. We are called to be a people, a people loved by God. We are sustained by God through one another. Whether married or single, we need to weave a network of support that will sustain us as well as celebrate with us.

Exercise: Spiritual Discipline

Rituals are a natural part of our lives. We often develop them without realizing it. When we don't have time for a particular act, we recognize that it has become an established event in our life. Most parents know what happens when they forget some part of the bedtime ritual for their young children. Rituals can also help us institute a change or recognize the importance of a decision. Not all rituals are carried out daily or even weekly. However, they gain power each time we do them. Eating together forms a ritual for Esther, Jennie, and Martha. Food is frequently an important part of a ritual. When we eat together, however simple the meal, we share what sustains us physically. When we pray together, we share what sustains us spiritually.

From time to time, you will want to renew the commitment you made in your mission statement. Preparing a ritual, one that you can adjust to your circumstances, can provide the way to do that. A family or group of friends may develop a ritual they can repeat on a regular basis. Consider including the following items in such a ritual, based on a list from Ernest Boyer's *A Way in the World: Family Life as Spiritual Discipline*:[2]

—Invite others to join you.
—Eat together.
—Include each person present in leadership.
—Pray, including prayers of gratitude as well as intercession.
—Celebrate your growth and changes.
—Design a symbol or symbolic act to repeat each time.
—Light candles.
—Enjoy the time together; don't solemnize the occasion.

Our friends, the Williamses, designed this ritual that they hold every two months:

—Family members, on a rotating basis, prepare the dining room table for the ritual. That family member chooses the decorations for the table and lights the candles later.
—Another family member prepares a simple dessert, such as ice cream sundaes, or bakes or purchases a favorite cookie.
—After eating together, the candles are lit.
—Then the family reads their mission statement in unison, followed by a time of silence for each one to think about how they have lived it over the past two months.
—After the silence, the conversation begins. During this time, they laugh and sometimes argue. They recall what they have done

to help Ethel Winter and what more could be done.
—When it is time to conclude this discussion, each family member is asked this question by the others, "Are you willing to continue with this ministry?"
—So far, they have always all answered yes, but the day may come when together they will need to revise their mission statement.
—The ritual is concluded with a time of prayer. The first two times they did this, the prayers were silent. More recently, the family members have prayed briefly aloud.
—The candles are extinguished and the ritual is concluded.

Each family or group of friends will find a different way to renew the commitment to their mission statement. As the circumstances for individuals change, the commitment will necessarily change. However, in order to attain the harmony of balancing personal, work, and church responsibilities, it is hoped that each person will continue to listen for that call from God.

A Closing Word

You, of course, are not finished with the work of balancing your personal, work, and church responsibilities even though you have read this book. The search for "perfect harmony" is a circular motion, not a vertical or horizontal one. We come full circle again and again throughout our lives. What you are doing now will change many times over, but we pray that each change will bring you closer to God and more in harmony with those persons most important to you. With Paul, we say to you, "As you therefore have received Christ Jesus the Lord, continue to live your lives in him, rooted and built up in him and established in the faith, just as you were taught, abounding in thanksgiving" (Col. 2:1–5).

LEADER'S
GUIDE

Introduction

—A mother of a teenager is trying to figure out how her child can be in both the confirmation or church membership class, which meets on Sunday morning, and on the traveling soccer team, which practices on Sunday morning.

—A single adult is now the long-distance caregiver for a mother who is clearly unable to handle her finances.

—A new church member meets his pastor in the grocery store. The church member turns beet red and mumbles something about a lot of business travel and needing Sundays for family time.

—One look at your calendar suggests that you will not be home any evening this week, unless you turn down a dinner invitation you have for Saturday night.

Who is this course for?

All the folks above and a whole lot more. Virtually every adult in our congregations—employed or retired, parent or not, married or single—is dealing with the tensions created by conflicts among personal and family responsibilities, work responsibilities, and church responsibilities. We live in a time of interests that clash and are surrounded by a multitude of choices about how to use our time. For many, leisure (if they have any) is as structured as a morning on the job. Few and far between are the persons in the church who could not benefit from entering into a discussion about time, responsibilities, and faith priorities, particularly with other Christians. An assumption behind this course is that such a conversation, certainly for Christians, needs to be based on a firm spiritual and faith foundation.

While this course is primarily for adults, there are suggestions for working at this issue as families. In this case, children who are younger than eight will probably be happier in a setting with their peers and caregivers or activity leaders. However, the children older than eight years are beginning to feel the tensions and need to be part of the solutions chosen by their family.

In this course, the participants will take note of the turmoil present in most lives today around the issues of home, work, and church. How can we be responsible and faithful persons in each realm? The process helps them identify their faith values and examine their lives with those values in mind. Then they will be encouraged to select an area that they want to change so they might live their faith values more fully. They will learn some skills to help this happen, develop ways to find support for the times when change is not so easy, and think about how they might provide support for others.

Early in your preparation for the course, take stock of your congregational life and the opportunities for supporting those who desire to make lifestyle changes. Where will they find models or mentors? What groups will honor their commitments? The final session is designed to help the participants select and plan ways to support one another in the process of change toward more faithful lives. Having a knowledge of existing resources will be an advantage. The bibliography in this book is a good place to start.

Who are the leaders?

You may be reading this guide because you have already agreed to lead this course. If so, consider your particular skills and these expectations of the leaders for this course:

— have experience in leading groups, particularly group discussion
— be willing to give direction, but not lectures
— have knowledge of the Bible and theology
— be able to serve as a mentor to other adults

If your first reaction to this list is, "What have I gotten myself into?" don't resign yet. Which of these skills do you have? Which ones do you lack? Talk with persons whose talents complement your skills. Recruit some of them to plan and lead the sessions with you. Draw on the strengths of each person. For example, if you are comfortable leading groups in discussion and other types of learning activities but feel you are limited in the areas of Bible and theology, find someone who can be a resource person—a scholar-in-residence for the course. Give that person a copy of this book. Ask her or him to read the materials and be prepared to help out in the Bible study, when a question of theological interpretation arises in the group, and to offer theological insight from time to time.

Or perhaps you are leading a group of parents, and while you have the other skills, you have never been a parent. Describe the course to one or two couples in the congregation who have raised their children and who are respected by others. Ask them to attend as participants and draw them into the discussions at appropriate times so they can describe their parenting experiences. Assure these assistants that it is not so much that they have the answers for others, but that they can empathize with younger parents and assure them that they can do this task or make the necessary change.

Perhaps you are reading this guide because you think it may be helpful for the adults in your church. As you ponder the matter of who will lead, think in the plural. The advantages of having a leadership team are many. Besides being able to meet all the criteria above, the dynamics of a leadership team will enrich the sessions, both as they are planned and led. The more diverse the leadership team is in terms of age, family, and background, the more individuals will see that the course is for them. Once the leadership team is recruited or called to this ministry, you may want to meet with them to help them begin their planning. Emphasize the importance of planning together and of the presence of each team member at every session.

The participants can share in the leadership tasks as well. If you have beverages and snacks, post a sign-up sheet for the participants to provide and/or be in charge of setting up the refreshments. Label a table as the "Other Resources" site, and invite the group to bring in newspaper and magazine articles, books, videos, and anything they have found that pertains to the topic of this course. Set aside a few minutes in each session, if you wish, to highlight what is on the table. A group member might lead group singing as you wait for the last of the group to arrive, or participants may take turns offering an opening prayer. The more involved each person is in the course, the more each will want to help the course to be successful for everyone.

Ways to use this course

In this day of multiple lifestyles and competing interests for our time, we can hardly provide any program resource with a single use or audience. A course like this needs to be adaptable in both the setting and the intended audience. Adapt the course to fit your group more closely. As a framework, each session is given in a one-hour format for a group of adults (married, single, parents, old, young, employed, retired, etc.). This basic design is supplemented with suggestions for groups of families as noted earlier, groups of parents with children at home, and for a retreat setting. The times allotted to the activities are merely approximate. The number of participants will vary the time in some instances, as will the amount of time they want to discuss a particular point.

While the time frame used in preparing these sessions was one hour, the sessions can easily be expanded to a one and one-half hour program by providing additional discussion time in one or more activities. Read all the ideas before selecting the one you will use, no matter what the composition of your group and the time frame. The particular dynamics of your group, the time and other resources available, and the leadership skills in your team may be better suited to one of the other activities suggested for a group different from yours.

Specific suggestions are given for a retreat weekend because such a condensed schedule will not allow time for the participants to try out the changes they identify. Thus, the adaptation for the retreat setting tries to take that setting into account, as well as the more relaxed atmosphere of being away from home. For this topic, it may be particularly important to help persons link up with others with similar concerns so they can support one another after the retreat. Here are two possible schedules for a weekend retreat:

—Friday evening: Everyone arrives and settles in, Session 1
—Saturday morning: Session 2

—Saturday afternoon: Session 3, with free time
—Saturday evening: Session 4 and an evening vesper or prayer time
—Sunday morning: Session 5, with a closing worship

OR

—Friday evening: Everyone arrives and settles in, Session 1
—Saturday morning: Session 2
—Saturday afternoon: Sessions 3 and 4 with a break between them
—Saturday evening: recreation and relaxation
—Sunday morning: Session 5, with a closing worship

Create an inviting environment

Any discussion group is enhanced by a warm, inviting room, but a discussion that asks the participants to think about the very warp and woof of their lives relies on an atmosphere of welcome that is immediately apparent. Here are some things to consider as you arrange the space:

—comfortable chairs that can be moved easily into various configurations for small groups
—good lighting, but not so bright that it tires eyes and brains
—a clean, uncluttered room
—soft music playing as the group enters
—nametags on the leaders and others ready for the participants
—table space for displays or writing by individuals or small groups
—What else would make the space feel inviting to you?

How are the sessions organized?

Each session is planned with the same five types of activities:

— Introduce the Session or Review the Previous Sessions
— Reflect on Your Faith
— Enter the Focus Question
— Examine Your Life
— Nurture Your Spiritual Life

The focus for each session is in the form of a question. That question provides the avenue for entering the session topic. You will find it at the beginning of each session plan and featured in the activity "Enter the Focus Question."

For each session, there is a brief Bible study called "Reflect on Your Faith." As you plan the sessions, take time to reflect on the Bible passage yourself and with your team. Look for connections between the rest of the session activities and the passage, and between your life and the passage. Anticipate how the participants might connect with the Bible passage.

"Enter the Focus Question" is a brief activity aimed at drawing the group into the topic. It provides ways for them to connect with the topic.

In "Examine Your Life," the participants looks more closely at their lives, their faith, and the specific issue. Generally, this activity will take the largest portion of the session.

Concluding each session is "Nurture Your Spiritual Life." This activity features a different spiritual discipline each time. Spiritual disciplines are those practices that keep us in touch with God. They can be practiced alone or with others, such as family members, housemates, or friends. An important source of support for making changes in your life, large or small, can be your connection to God. That connection is strengthened through the kinds of spiritual practices or disciplines found in this course.

You will notice that there are some pages in each session that can be photocopied for the group. Please note that these are the only pages that you have permission to photocopy. Each of these pages is clearly identified with that permission.

With each activity is a list of materials needed. Generally, these items will be easily found in stationery or craft stores.

The participant's book

Before you plan the sessions, skim or read quickly through the participant's section of this book to get a general idea of what it contains. Then, as you plan each session, read the chapter related to that session more carefully. You may find topics or examples in your reading that will be especially pertinent to your group.

While *you* will read the chapter before the session, the *participants* are not expected to read that chapter until *after* the session. Therefore, you do *not* need to get the books to them before the course begins. The book will serve as a review, provide more information on the topic, and become a reminder for them to do the homework or assignment related to the session.

It may be that some persons will read the entire participant's book as soon as they get it. That's fine; rejoice at their keen interest. It is also possible that someone who cannot attend the course will read the book and work on his or her own. The book is written to be used by individuals in this way as well. However, these persons will not have the support of others in making changes that are likely to be counter to the prevailing culture. The help of such support cannot be underestimated. You might want to invite such persons to any gatherings or other offerings in this area following the course.

A word to the wise

If you do not usually provide childcare for parents when a course is offered other than Sunday morning, think about doing it for this study. Providing such care says clearly to the parents that the church is concerned about them and wants to help them find new patterns for their lives. If you want to help parents make important changes in their busy lives, get them together to talk about such changes. Provide help to get over the roadblocks, tiny and big, along the way. Child care may be all that is needed for many parents to attend.

Get the word around

How will you let people know this study is happening? Use every means available to you. Announce it in newsletters, special mailings, and during the announcements time at the service of worship. Post flyers and posters. Then recruit a core group so the course will be sure to happen. Tap into the needs you hear expressed for slowing down or spending more time with the family. Be clear about what the course will help them do and the extent of the commitment you deem necessary.

Follow-up

Think about what will come after the course before you offer it. What options are already available that could be seen as follow-up to this course, such as fellowship groups, extended family groups, parenting groups, faith and work groups? While you need not have another program or group ready to hand them at the last session, know what resources are already at hand.

Tasks to complete before the first session

—Make the overhead transparencies for the sessions. Check the overhead projector to see that it works and determine where you will place it in the room. If a projector is not available, photocopy the page and enlarge to create a poster.

—Call or send notes to those who are coming to express your pleasure that they will be in the group.

—Read the participant's book.

Session One
The Foundation of Your Life

Focus question: What are my core commitments?

In this session, the participants will explore how the balancing of personal, family, work, and church responsibilities is a spiritual issue, a matter of faithful living. They will begin by determining their core commitments, particularly those values that help them live out their faith. Day-to-day living is based on these commitments. This section offers participants self-assessments, discussion, small group activities, and follow-up assignments. These activities provide the basis for examining lives and for making changes, a constant theme in this course.

Because this is the opening session, have nametag supplies ready. If even one person does not know the other participants, nametags are a helpful feature.

Session Outline (60 minutes)

1. Introduce the Course
   10–15 minutes

2. Reflect on Your Faith
   15 minutes

3. Enter the Focus Question
   5 minutes

4. Examine Your Life
20 minutes

5. Nurture Your Spiritual Life
10 minutes

To Prepare for This Session

—Set out nametags and markers for the participants. Have nametags for the leaders too.
—Arrange the chairs for the first activity.
—Post a sign with the focus question for this session where everyone will be able to see it.
—Before the participants arrive, pray for God's Spirit to assist you and to be present during the session. Pray your breath prayer (see Activity 5).

Activity 1
Introduce the Course

Goal: To introduce the participants to one another and to the topic

Materials: Nametags, markers, masking tape

If the participants do not know one another, select an appropriate activity for getting acquainted from the suggestions below for the opening moments for the various audiences. Even if many of them are acquainted, this activity is a good way to learn new things about one another. When preparing to discuss such important issues as core commitments and how to change one's life, an atmosphere of trust and familiarity is helpful. One activity cannot build that atmosphere,

but it can certainly help to set the tone.

After the introductions are made, proceed to introduce the topic.

Place a line of masking tape on the floor from one wall to the opposite wall, moving any furniture away from it. Ask the group to stand. Explain that you are going to read several sentences, one at a time. They are to stand on the tape according to their agreement or disagreement with the statement. Point to one end of the tape and call it "I definitely, without a doubt, agree" and the opposite end of the tape, "I couldn't disagree with that statement any more if you paid me." The participants are to stand anywhere along the tape that corresponds with how they feel about the sentence you read. Begin with these sentences, adding others or changing them as you deem appropriate for your group:

—My favorite time of the year is winter.
—I think chocolate is the perfect food.
—My checkbook balances every month, without using a computer program.
—Getting here for this program was a breeze.
—Life gets easier as I get older.
—I would rather go to the beach than to the mountains.
—I have at least one favorite TV show that I try to watch every week.
—My work and personal life rarely conflict.

When the participants have found places to stand after a statement, ask two or three at different places on the tape to say why they chose that spot. Or have those standing near one another talk together. People frequently chose a point for differing reasons. This will give them conversation entry points during the break or other times when they meet.

Next, explain the purpose of this course in your own words, adapting the following to the way you have planned the course:

"This course is for Christians who are seeking to live faithfully in their personal lives, their work lives, and their church lives. Responsibilities in these three areas sometimes conflict and create tension. This tension changes daily, weekly, and yearly as circumstances in any area of life vary. One's faith or spiritual life can be the foundation on which the efforts to resolve the conflict and ease the tension or transform it to a creative tension are built. For that to happen, one's spiritual life must be nurtured regularly."

Describe the way you have organized the course and provide any other information the participants may need, such as "get refreshments as you wish" or "we will begin promptly, so try to be on time."

Show the group the participant's book and explain that it will be distributed at the conclusion of this session, or however you have planned to provide it for them.

Keep this introduction brief, especially if you are leading a group of families.

For groups of families

As families arrive, explain that they are to plan a way to introduce themselves to the others in a two-minute skit, TV ad, or whatever they devise. When all the families are ready or the time has come to begin the presentations, bring everyone together. Keep the pace moving quickly during the presentations so that it does not take too much time.

Although this activity is more time-consuming that the other suggestions, having each family work together in a fun task reminds them that family cooperation can be a good thing—an important concept for this course.

For groups of parents

Ask each person to describe her or his family in three words that begin with one of her or his initials. For example, Lily Masters might say, "My name is Lily Masters. My family is laughing, literate, and loving." When they are ready, have them stand, one at a time, to say their names and the three words chosen.

In retreat settings

In a more relaxed setting, take more time for getting acquainted. Distribute three index cards and a pen to each person. Have them write three things about themselves on the three cards, one to a card, trying to think of things that the others will not know. Ask them to place the cards face down on a large table as they finish. When everyone's cards are on the table, have each person take three cards (but they cannot keep their own cards). They are to find the authors of the three cards and have them sign their cards. Display the cards for the group to read throughout the event.

If the retreat is an intergenerational group, ask the participants to draw three things or act out something about themselves before the entire group.

Activity 2
Reflect on Your Faith

Goal: To reflect on how God calls us to faithfulness

Materials: Bibles

Two Bible passages especially pertinent to considering how we live faithfully, whatever our family configuration, are Deuteronomy 32:44–47 and Micah 6:6–8. As you prepare for this activity, read about these passages in chapter 1.

Introduce Deuteronomy 32:44–47 by noting that Moses is speaking to the whole community here, not just the parents of dependent children. The adult community is responsible for telling and showing the word of God to the children. Thus, each adult bears responsibility for reflecting on her or his life and the values it exhibits. Ask a participant to read verses 46–47 aloud. Ask for reactions and comments.

Then introduce Micah 6:6–8 by explaining that Micah was a prophet during the eighth century B.C.E. Some scholars see these verses as the sum of the Hebraic covenant law. These verses may provide the basis for our core commitments. They may provide a yardstick by which we

measure our faithfulness to God's covenant. Again ask for reactions and comments.

Finally ask, "How do these two passages complement each other or work together? What do they suggest about the priorities and commitments we ought to have as Christian disciples, people of God?"

For groups of families

Materials: Bibles, newsprint, markers, masking tape, music and words for "What Does the Lord Require of You?" or another song based on Micah 6:6–8

Gather in family groups. Smaller family groups might combine to make larger groups, but not larger than seven persons. Discovering that two families can work together is another good learning. Read Micah 6:6–8 aloud in each group.

In the same groups, brainstorm ways that Christians do each of these things (do justice, love kindness, walk humbly with God) individually, as families, and as a congregation of believers. Have the groups keep track of their ideas on newsprint. Post the newsprint sheets as each group reports, naming only those ideas that have not already been named.

Then sing "What Does God Require of You?" by Jim Strathdee, found in *The Chalice Hymnal* (Chalice Press, 1995) and *The Book of Praise* (Presbyterian Church in Canada, 1997), or look in your congregation's hymnal for another hymn based on Micah 6:6–8.

For groups of parents

Materials: Bibles

Read both passages but look particularly at the Deuteronomy passage. Form groups of three or four persons each and have them discuss the meaning of Moses' words to them in their role as parent. Where do they find or seek help to parent their children? How is the community of faith involved in that parenting and nurturing? How else might it contribute?

In retreat settings

Materials: banner fabric, paper, pencils, fabric remnants, yarn, scissors, glue, masking tape or tacks

If the weather and setting are appropriate, go outdoors to read the Scripture passages. Sit under a tree to hear the words of Moses and stand in a public place (perhaps the porch by the dining hall) to hear those of Micah.

Make banners that promote doing justice, loving kindness, and walking humbly with God. Form three groups (or more with a large number of participants) and assign each group one of the requirements in Micah 6. Provide each group with a piece of sturdy fabric, such as felt or denim, three or four feet long. Give them paper and pencils to design the banners before attaching anything to the fabric. Large designs work better than detailed ones. Provide fabric remnants, yarn, scissors, and glue for each group. Tack or tape the banners to the walls of the room where you are meeting.

Activity 3
Enter the Focus Question

Goal: To introduce the topic specific to this session, "What are my core commitments?"

Materials: writing paper and pencils

Introduce this activity by explaining "core commitments;" those ideals that we hold most dear and that undergird our faith. Many people operate out of a set of values that they simply took from their family, without examining them. Others examined the values they were raised with and rejected many of them. As adults, an examination of our core commitments is in order on a regular basis, because our loyalties may shift away from the values that we intend to live by as we try to balance the demands of work, church, family, and our own needs. Then, the anchor that centers us may be loose and we feel as though we are floating from one thing to the next, perhaps crashing into others and the shore.

There are many ways to discover the commitments we use for daily living. One way is to write down those that are important to you. Provide a piece of paper and pencils for the group. Have them fold the paper lengthwise. Ask them on one side to list the things that are most important to them, for example, "the family gathering on holidays," "involvement in a project that helps others," or "spending time with close friends."

Another way is to recall the messages or sayings that we grew up with and that we may continue to repeat or hear in our subconscious. Some are:

—If it is worth doing, it is worth doing right.
—The early bird gets the worm.
—You made your bed; now you have to lie in it.
—I didn't raise a quitter.
—The family that prays together stays together.

Ask the group members to find partners (not a spouse or family member) and recall the messages and sayings in their backgrounds. After they have talked for about five minutes, have them examine the messages they recall and name the commitments that are behind them.

Then have them list the commitments from this activity on the opposite side of the paper on which they wrote the things important to them earlier. However, they are not to open the sheet of paper.

For groups of families

Materials: photocopies of the family shield (page 67), markers or crayons

Create family shields. Give each family a copy of the shield, a pencil, and markers or crayons. Suggest this process:

—On the back of the paper, list the things and ideas that are important to your family.
—Select four of the most important. This should be done by consensus.
—In each section of the shield,

draw or write something about one of these important things or ideas.
—Decorate your shield with the markers or crayons, if you like, and print your family names around the shield.

When all the family shields are completed, have a parade with each family carrying their shield. Lead the parade so the participants double back and can see the other shields. At the end of the session, collect the shields so they will be available for Session 2, Activity 1.

For groups of parents

Materials: writing paper and pencils

Referring to the Deuteronomy passage, ask the group to reflect first on the memories they have of their childhood. What stands out? What persons are central to those memories? What values are key to those events and persons?

Then, have them think quietly for a moment about the memories they want their children, grandchildren, and future generations to have. Try to keep their focus ever expanding to the children beyond their immediate family or extended family. As the words of Moses suggest, they are to look after all the children. Remind them of the vows made in infant baptism or dedication, particularly the promise of the congregation to help the family nurture the faith of this little one.

Have the parents individually write the memories they want for their children. Suggest that they be as specific as they can, even saying what they might hope for each child. Then in groups of three or four, they can look for the values implicit in those memories.

In retreat settings

Materials: colored card stock, markers, scissors, pencils, glue, and masking tape or safety pins

Have the participants spend time alone recalling childhood memories and reflecting on the values derived from them.

Make available colored card stock, markers, scissors, pencils, and glue for each participant to create a personal button (about 6–8 inches in diameter) that suggests the commitments most important to them. The buttons can be worn by attaching them with safety pins or masking tape to their clothing. The buttons will be good conversation starters during meals and free time.

If there are children and young people present, suggest that they think of something they have done with their family that is a good memory. This can be the focus of their buttons.

Activity 4
Examine Your Life

Goal: To begin identifying places where the balance of responsibilities is one-sided or otherwise out of sync

Materials: overhead projector and "Symbol" transparency (page 68)

Continue working with the previous activity by asking,

—Which commitments on the two lists are the same or close to the same?

—Which appear to be contradictory or conflicting?

—Which values (on either list) are practiced in your work environment?

—Are these values that constitute success for you? In your family life? At work? As a disciple of Jesus Christ? Why or why not?

—How do these values support your faith? How do they fit with the words from Moses or Micah read earlier?

—What are the barriers from any part of your life that stop you from following through on your core commitments? What are your fears? Where do you find support?

—Display the "Symbol" overhead transparency. What does this symbol say to you about your commitments, your life, and your faith?

This discussion will not be concluded in this session. Therefore, suggest that the participants continue to ponder these questions during the days ahead. Ask them, before the next session, to write, in no more than one paragraph, their personal or, if married, family mission statement. See chapter 1 for more on such mission statements. They are to bring what they have prepared, even if in a draft stage, to the next session. They will have additional material to consider if they read the introduction and chapter 1 before the next session.

For groups of families

Materials: family shields, papers with the questions, overhead projector, "Symbol" transparency (page 68)

Have each family sit in a circle with their shield on the floor or table in the middle. Ask them to discuss these questions that you have printed on papers for each group:

—When do these commitments help us live together?
—When do they get in the way of what we want to do or create disagreements in our family?

After the families have had time to get into this discussion, call everyone together. Remind them that every family has times when commitments and wants clash. How we work together to resolve those clashes is what this course is about. Project the "Symbol" transparency. Explain that as Christians we look to our faith as a way to help us find strength and to resolve problems. This prepares the group for Activity 5.

Now or at the end of Activity 5, ask the parents to read the introduction and chapter 1 in the participant's section and, as a family, work on a mission statement to bring to the next session.

For groups of parents

Materials: overhead projector, "Symbol" transparency (page 68)

Have each participant review the commitments discovered in the mem-

ories they desire for their children and what creates tension in trying to provide those memories. Assure them that this tension is quite normal.

Project the "Symbol" transparency. Explain that this course is about how we try to balance the tension among personal or family, work, and church responsibilities to create a life that is faithful to God's covenant. Thus, in the week ahead they may want to ponder how their desired memories fit into that faithfulness. Assign the introduction and chapter 1. Ask them to pay particular attention to the section on mission statements, and to write one to bring to the next session.

In retreat settings

You may be able to spend more time in this discussion. Begin by having each person interpret his or her button. For a large group, form groups of three or four persons to do this. Then, discuss values and commitments more generally, using the questions from the basic activity plan above.

Distribute the books to participants and refer the group to the section on personal and family mission statements. Suggest that they begin drafting such a statement for themselves.

Activity 5
Nurture Your Spiritual Life

Goal: To learn about breath prayer

Materials: overhead projector, "Symbol" transparency, copies of "Words and Phrases for Breath Prayers" (page 66)

Noting the symbol on the transparency, say that the nurturing of our faith is so important that each session will conclude with the explanation and practice of a spiritual discipline. The spiritual discipline for this session is the breath prayer. This simple prayer can be used by all ages at any time and in any place. Dating back many years, the breath prayer is said as you breathe in and out.

Distribute the handout, "Words and Phrases for Breath Prayers." Select a phrase or word from the list and practice the breath prayer together. Sit comfortably. Breathe in deeply and say or think the first syllable or phrase. As you release your breath, say or think the last syllable or phrase.

People young and old have prayed this way as they have sat in their cars at a traffic light, stood in line at the grocery store, watched for a bus, waited anxiously for a test to begin, or dealt with a conflict at work. The deep breathing and the comforting words bring you to your center, where God is waiting for you. When you feel the tensions of your life becoming overbearing, pause for a moment or two with your breath prayer. This may help you look at the situation with clearer eyes and a calmer spirit.

Suggest that the participants practice their breath prayers daily until the next session. Conclude with the following prayer or one of your own: God of all life, be with each one here during the days ahead. Slow us down and turn our eyes to you. In Jesus' name. Amen.

For groups of families

Materials: overhead projector, "Symbol" transparency, copies of "Words and Phrases for Breath Prayers" (page 66)

Have each family select a breath prayer and practice it together. Suggest that they begin by saying it softly as they search for a rhythm that is comfortable for everyone. Their breath prayer can be the opening for a mealtime prayer or a way they remind one another to slow down and be with God.

For groups of parents

Materials: overhead projector, "Symbol" transparency, copies of "Words and Phrases for Breath Prayers" (page 66)

The breath prayer is helpful to many parents as a way to stop themselves from reacting in anger. Suggest that they teach it to their children as well.

In retreat settings

Materials: overhead projector, "Symbol" transparency, copies of "Words and Phrases for Breath Prayers" (page 66)

Give the directions for a breath prayer. Then have the participants find their own places in the retreat center to practice the prayer they have chosen. Suggest that they look for a place that they can return to whenever they wish to pray or reflect on God and what is taking place at the retreat.

Words and Phrases for Breath Prayers

Je/sus

Jesus/loves me.

Come/Lord Jesus.

The Lord/is my shepherd.

Be still and know/that I am God.

I am with you/always.

Come/Holy Spirit.

God's steadfast love/endures forever.

Bless the Lord/O my soul.

Christ is/our peace.

Make room/in my heart.

Say or think the first syllable or phrase as you breathe in. Say or think the last syllable or phrase as you release your breath slowly. Repeat this process with each breath.

The word or phrase that fits you today will not always fit. Keep this list and be alert to phrases in the Bible and in hymns that can be breath prayers for you in the future.

Permission is granted for the leader to copy this page for distribution to the participants in the group.

Family Shield

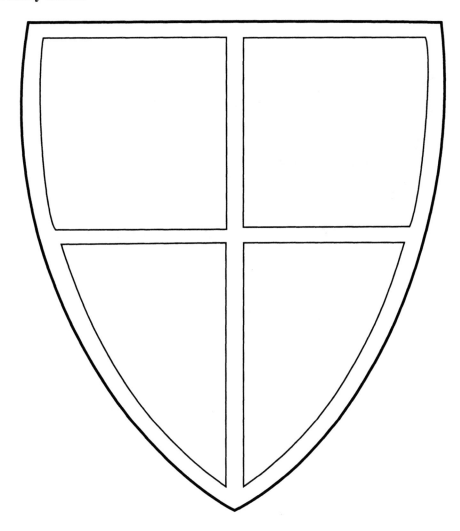

Symbol

Permission is granted for the leader to copy this page for distribution to the participants for use as an overhead transparency.

Session Two
Not Enough Time, Too Many Choices

Focus Question: How do my commitments help me use my time and make choices that are consistent with my faith?

After reviewing the material for Session 1, the participants will examine two realities everyone encounters—time and choices—and explore how the decisions regarding them are made and might be changed. Time is a given; it is divided into hours, days, weeks, and years. Choices, however, come by the multitudes, if we can be creative in recognizing them.

One intent of this course is to help the participants see choices they had not seen before. Even choices that are not viable may lead us to discovering still more choices. An advantage of talking with others in a study like this is that frequently others see options that our minds and eyes have not seen.

Together, time and choices constitute a significant portion of how we make decisions about living our faith commitments. This session will lead the participants on a never-ending path of considering their decisions in light of the time they have and the wide range of choices before them, and doing this in light of the personal or family mission statements they have written.

Session Outline (60 minutes)

1. Review the Previous Session
   5–10 minutes

2. Reflect on Your Faith
   15 minutes

3. Enter the Focus Question
   5–10 minutes

4. Examine Your Life
   20 minutes

5. Nurture Your Spiritual Life
   10 minutes

To Prepare for This Session

—Display a poster with the focus question for this session where everyone will be able to see it.
—Arrange the room for the first activity.
—Have nametags available if any members of the group do not know the others.
—Before the participants begin to arrive, pray for God's presence. Also pray your breath prayer.

Activity 1
Review the Previous Session

Goal: To recall the main points of Session 1 and hear the participants' insights and questions from their reading and thinking

Materials: overhead projector, "Symbol" transparency from Session 1

Show the overhead transparency of the symbol of how we try to balance our personal, work, and church responsibilities. Ask the group to describe their experience with the breath prayer, as well as any insights they had into the topics from the first session or questions that have come to them since then. It is not necessary now to discuss their mission statements. While you may not be able to answer or discuss in this session the questions raised, write them down so they may be addressed in another session. If some questions will not be included in this course, provide the names of some other resources to the persons raising those questions. If you have a resource table, such resources can be added to it.

Conclude this activity by asking the group, "What did you discover about the two lists of commitments that you made in the previous session?" Not everyone will want to answer the question aloud, but posing the question will help the group enter the topic for this session.

For groups of families

Materials: family shields from Session 1

After reviewing the main points from Session 1, distribute the family shields made then. Have each family stand, one at a time. They are to introduce themselves like this: "We are (each one says his or her full name). Our family shield shows (name the subject of each section of the shield)."

For groups of parents

Materials: overhead projector, "Symbol" transparency from Session 1

Review the main points from Session 1 as described above. Then have the group recall the memories they desire for their children. Did they have any new thoughts about those memories since the first session? What about the implicit values they saw in those memories? As they have thought about this, are there memories that they have already provided for their children without realizing it? Ask for comments and questions regarding the introduction and chapter 1.

In retreat settings

While you may not need to spend as much time in reviewing the previous session in a retreat setting, where the sessions follow one another more closely, do include an opportunity for the group to express new insights or ask questions that have come to them during the free time. If this is an intergenerational retreat, invite comments from all ages.

Activity 2
Reflect on Your Faith

Goal: To consider the implications of viewing time as a gift of God

Materials: Bibles

See that each participant has a Bible. Ask them to turn to Ecclesiastes 3:1–15 and read it silently, looking for points when it connects with their lives today.

When they have had time to read and reflect, point out that this book of the Bible has been described as a book that tells us how to cope with life when the world does not make sense. One message from this philosopher

writer is that nothing in life is static. Ask, "How does 3:1–15 give this message? What other messages do you take from this passage?"

We have a specifically Christian message regarding change and struggle in 2 Corinthians 4:7–10. Read these verses aloud. Ask, "What provides the hope in this passage? How is it different from the message in Ecclesiastes? Together, how do you find them a source of God's presence?"

Conclude this discussion by noting that each change in our life offers a new set of choices and new decisions to make. The message of hope for us is that no matter what the struggle or change, God is with us.

For groups of families

Materials: Bible, newsprint, markers, masking tape

After reading Ecclesiastes 3:1–15, provide each family with two sheets of newsprint and markers. Ask them to list important events in the life of their family on one sheet. As the leader, be aware that for some, perhaps most, families, making this list will bring some major tragedy to the emotional surface. Be supportive when this pain is recalled and felt. Try not to minimize it as only an experience of the past.

When they have listed these events, they can use the other sheet to compile their list into a prayer in a style similar to that of Ecclesiastes 3:2–8. For example, the following list:

—marriage of the parents
—birth of first child
—move to present location

—death of grandparent
—birth of second child
—first child falls and breaks arm

might become:

For everything there is a season, and for our family there is a time for every matter under heaven:
a time to be single, and a time to be married;
a time to celebrate the birth of our children, and
a time to celebrate the lives of our grandparents

As they finish their family histories, each family member can sign the history. Tape the family histories to a wall or room divider.

To conclude this activity, remind the group that through each of these times, God was with them, even when they could not feel God's presence.

For groups of parents

Materials: Bibles, writing paper, pens

After reading Ecclesiastes 3:1–15 aloud or silently, ask the group to reflect on the changes in their lives since becoming parents. Discuss this together, so each person's thinking is enriched and enlarged. Then read 2 Corinthians 4:8–10 and discuss its impact on their thinking. After this discussion, provide writing paper and pens and have the group write letters to their children describing the changes they have experienced and expressing their trust in God through these changes or how they see such changes as a part of God's providence now.

If their children are old enough, they can give the letter to them. If not, suggest that they save their letters to give to their children at an appropriate time.

In retreat settings

Materials: photocopies of "Choral Reading" (page 77)

Photocopy the choral reading (page 77), one for each participant. Form two groups, Group A and Group B. Ask the groups to rehearse their parts alone before reading the passage together. Encourage them to add movements and to read their parts dramatically. When they are ready, read the passage together. Then ask the two groups to stand in opposite corners of the room or an outdoor area. As they read their sections of Ecclesiastes 3:2–8, have them move toward each other. When they get to verses 11–15, they should be one group and read those verses in unison.

Discuss the passage, using the questions in the basic activity above.

Activity 3
Enter the Focus Question

Goal: To deliberate on how to use time and to make choices so that they are consistent with one's faith values

Materials: overhead projector, "Time and Choices" transparency, plain paper, pencils (page 78)

Display the overhead transparency "Time and Choices." Introduce this activity with the following points about time:

—No matter where you are in the life cycle, it seems there is not enough time. Ask active retirees, and they will tell you they do not have enough time. Ask new parents, and they will say that time has taken on a new dimension. Ask adolescents, and they will tell you about their busy schedules. A classic book for caregivers of persons with Alzheimer's disease is titled *The Thirty-six Hour Day,* a poignant reminder of the continuous responsibility of these caregivers.

—You may long for more time, but you're not likely to get it. Therefore, what counts is not the amount of time you have, but how you choose to use that time.

—Requests for your time will come from many quarters, especially family members, your employer or work, and your congregation. When someone asks something of you, you must determine whether or not to say yes. If you are certain about what is important to you (commitments and faith), you will have a basis on which to make that decision. Every request for your time deserves consideration before you answer. Guilt should not be the motivating factor.

—While time is a given quantity, the number of choices that we have seems to explode year after year. Still, we can better consider those choices when we know how we are actually using our time and recognize the responsibilities that are non-negotiable.

Provide each participant with a sheet of plain paper and a pencil. Ask them to draw a large circle on the paper, one that fills the page. Then have them create a pie chart that shows how they spend their time. They should include family, personal, work, and church, although they may add other categories as well, thinking of the roles they fulfill. A sample pie chart of this type is in chapter 2. Assure them that this is not to be completely accurate, but is meant to help them gain a sense of the proportion given to each category.

When they have finished, ask them to turn to a partner and compare their charts. Urge them to look at the questions their allotment raises as they consider the values they identified in the previous session and the mission statement they wrote between sessions. Suggest that they write those questions on the back of the chart.

For groups of families

Materials: writing paper, pens or pencils

Briefly introduce the idea of time and choices above. Distribute paper and pens. Have each family group list the choices they made, alone or with other family members, during the past week or month. When their lists are finished, they are ready to move to Activity 4.

For groups of parents

Materials: photocopies of "One Day at a Time," (page 79) pencils

When a group of parents gather, talk of personal responsibilities quickly moves to talk of parenting responsibilities, including home-making responsibilities. Distribute copies of "One Day at a Time" and pencils.

Central to their realization about the use of this portion of their time is the importance of involving others (spouse, other family members, friends, church members) in the parenting responsibilities and household tasks, as well as releasing themselves from the guilt of not being the perfect parent. Refer to "The Good Enough Parent" (chapter 2) in the participant's section as you examine these responsibilities together.

This discussion should lead naturally into Activity 4, "A Way to Examine Your Life."

In retreat settings

Materials: plain paper, pencils or pens

Without much introduction, have the participants make the pie chart as described in the basic activity above. If this is a family retreat, the pie chart is a good activity for them to work on together. They may make individual pie charts later, but this one should show how they spend their time as a family.

When they have finished, introduce the idea of time as a limited quantity. Then, have the group think about how time has a different quality when they are in a retreat setting than when they are at home or at work. Time does not change, but what does? How might such changes

affect their life at home? Here, introduce the concept of Sabbath, a time that is spent in re-creation. See chapters 2 and 3.

Activity 4
Examine Your Life

Goal: To examine and evaluate how you make choices and use time

Materials: individual pie charts, photocopies of "One Day at a Time," (page 79), pencils, seven copies of "One Day at a Time" for each participant to take home

Have the participants look at their pie charts as you ask the following questions, allowing time for them to think but not speak aloud:

—What factors determine my use of time, such as age of my children, health of my family members, work tasks, household chores?
—Which of these pie wedges are larger than I want them to be?
—Which of these wedges are smaller than I want them to be?
—Which of these wedges is about the size I want it to be?
—How does my pie chart show the values I identified in the previous session and the mission statement I have written?

After this time for individual reflection, ask the group to identify, in general terms, what they discovered. Then ask them to design a perfect day, or at least a good enough day, according to their commitments. Distribute copies of "One Day at a Time" and pencils.

Explain that one goal of this exercise is to discover what a day would look like if it both exhibited their commitments and took into account the realities of their situation. Note that not every day has the same potential or perimeters. A workday would look different from a weekend day. A day in January might look different from one in August. Give a personal example of a change you have made as a result of preparing to lead this course or one you are working on at the moment.

Now or later, assign chapter 2 and ask each person to select possible areas for change in their lives to bring to the next session.

For groups of families

Materials: family shields, family mission statements

Ask the families to look at the lists of decisions they made in Activity 3 and discuss these questions:

—Which decisions had to do with time and how it is used?
—What did we consider as we made each decision?
—How do our decisions reflect the commitments we put on our family shield?
—How might we change the way we make decisions to take our commitments and our family mission statement into fuller account?

Invite any comments on the process before moving to Activity 5.

Now or later, ask the parents to read chapter 2, and ask each family to identify one or more areas for change for them before the next session.

For groups of parents

An important part of the memories we give our children is the ways they perceive us, their parents. These perceptions become the models they hold for being a spouse and a parent. Ask, "How do you want your children to remember you? Are your expectations of yourself as caregiver, parent, wife or husband, realistic, especially given the responsibilities you have in the home, your family, and your church? How are these expectations reflected in your family mission statement? What needs adjusting: your expectations or the statement?"

For the next session, ask the group to read chapter 2 and select possible areas in their life for change.

In retreat settings

Materials: photocopies of "One Day at a Time," (page 79), pencils

Give each person seven copies of "One Day at a Time" and a pencil. Ask them to complete the forms for a week, based on what they can recall of the previous week. Be sure they include the weekend. Once they have done this, ask them to look at the week with these questions in mind: How does what I did last week relate to my understanding of success? How does it connect with my commitments and faith? They might discuss this with a partner. On their own, ask them to ponder, How might I alter the ways I use time and the choices I make to better fit what I believe to be my commitments and faith?

Activity 5
Nurture Your Spiritual Life

Goal: To learn a daily method of self-examination and prayer

Materials: Bible

Read Ecclesiastes 3:1–2. Then introduce the spiritual discipline, the *examen*. The *examen* is an ancient method of offering our life to God, one day at a time. Through it you look at both the good and bad of the day or time period you are examining. Although the *examen* is usually done at the end of the day, at bedtime, you can use it anytime. The wonderful thing is that regular use of the *examen* can reveal the ways that God is working in our lives, pushing or leading us.

Have the group members find partners. While the *examen* can be done alone, it is particularly helpful to have someone who listens to you over time, often hearing what you do not hear and noting trends you have missed. Follow these steps:

—In your own mind, go over this day. What from it are you the most grateful to God? Name that moment for your partner.
—In your own mind, go over this day again. What from it are you least grateful to God? Name that moment for your partner.
—As you think about the moment

for which you were least grateful, you may discover that you chose that moment because of something you did or said. Ask God's forgiveness. Perhaps it was a moment when you felt wronged; ask God to help you forgive the other person.
—Pray, giving thanks to God for the moment for which you are most grateful. Try to keep that moment in your heart as you go forth or, at home, as you go to sleep.

For groups of families

Examen done as a family can bring out the strengths of family life. See the directions above. As each family member names the moments for which she or he is most and least thankful, each one's personality and faith is revealed, nurturing the faith of the other family members. Have the family do this together. Suggest that they do this each night, as often as possible.

For groups of parents

Have the parents follow the *examen* process above as couples or with someone else. Describe how this can be done with their children, drawing from the activity for families above.

In retreat settings

Explain the process of the *examen*. Take the group through the steps above, using the time they have been at the retreat setting as the time period. Then, suggest that they do the *examen* at bedtime, alone or with a partner.

Choral Reading

Everyone: For everything there is a season, and a time for every matter under heaven;

Group A: a time to be born,

Group B: and a time to die;

Group A: a time to plant,

Group B: and a time to pluck up what is planted;

Group A: a time to kill,

Group B: and a time to heal;

Group A: a time to break down,

Group B: and a time to build up;

Group A: a time to weep,

Group B: and a time to laugh;

Group A: a time to mourn,

Group B: and a time to dance;

Group A: a time to throw away stones,

Group B: and a time to gather stones together;

Group A: a time to embrace,

Group B: and a time to refrain from embracing;

Group A: a time to seek,

Group B: and a time to lose;

Group A: a time to keep,

Group B: and a time to throw away;

Group A: a time to tear,

Group B: and a time to sew;

Group A: a time to keep silence,

Group B: and a time to speak;

Group A: a time to love,

Group B: and a time to hate;

Group A: a time for war,

Group B: and a time for peace (Eccl. 3:1–8).

Group A: We often suffer, but we are never crushed.

Group B: Even when we don't know what to do, we never give up.

Group A: In times of trouble, God is with us,

Group B: and when we are knocked down, we get up again (2 Cor. 4:8–9 CEV).

Everyone: Can anything separate us from the love of Christ? Nothing in all creation can separate us from God's love for us in Christ Jesus our Lord! (Rom. 8:35a, 39b CEV).

Time and Choices

One Day at a Time

Session Three
Moving Ahead

Focus question: How do I select one area for change and solicit the support needed from others?

While determining one's faith values and examining one's life—the themes of Sessions 1 and 2—may be difficult, this session moves the participants into the area that involves more than the intellect. The previous sessions have set the stage for change. However, change, particularly constructive change, rarely happens on its own. To achieve a more faithful balance among personal and family, work, and church responsibilities, the participants will be asked to select an area for change and begin to plan for that alteration in their lives.

Session Outline (60 minutes)

1. Review the Previous Sessions
   5–10 minutes

2. Reflect on Your Faith
   15 minutes

3. Enter the Focus Question
   5–10 minutes

4. Prepare for Change
   25 minutes

5. Nurture Your Spiritual Life
   5 minutes

To Prepare for This Session

—Make photocopies of "Intercessory Prayer"(page 89) for the participants.
—Prepare a transparency of "Ripples" (page 90).
—If possible, display a print of Van Gogh's "The Sowers," available in the *Imaging the Word Poster Set 2* (United Church Press).

Activity 1
Review the Previous Sessions

Goal: To review the main points of the previous sessions and to hear participants' comments on their experiences since Session 2

Materials: paper, pencils

Briefly recall the main points covered in Sessions 1 and 2, such as:

—Living faithfully involves balancing personal or family, work, and church responsibilities.
—To live faithfully, we must determine the commitments that help this to happen.
—Time is a gift from God, but it is a finite gift; we cannot create more of it.
—Although time is finite, the choices about using that time are multiple, limited only by our creativity and abilities.

Ask the group to offer insights and questions that have come to them since Session 2. Write down the questions to address in future sessions, or

for which you might provide additional resources. Also inquire about their use of the spiritual discipline, *examen*. Hearing about the successes as well as the difficulties of others can be an affirmation of our own efforts.

For groups of families

Materials: overhead projector, transparencies for Sessions 1 and 2

Review briefly the points above, noting the activities that the group did in the first two sessions. For younger participants, the reminders about activities will probably be easier to recall than the more abstract main points. Another aid to their recall is the transparencies used in each session. Show the "Symbol" transparency as you read or paraphrase the first two points, and the "Time and Choices" transparency during the last two points.

For groups of parents

Materials: paper, pencils

Use the basic activity above. Especially seek their questions and comments as these points relate to parenting and family life. Ask about their use of *examen* with their children. Hearing about other families, even when the ages of the children are different, produces a touch of reality for all parents present . . . and often adds a moment of humor.

In retreat settings

Materials: newsprint, markers, masking tape

Rather than review the main points, print them attractively on newsprint and post them in the meeting space. This can be done by a group member talented in lettering or calligraphy. Then, the points will be before the group as they meet, and you can draw attention to them without having a formal review. Always ask for thoughts or questions that have come since the last group meeting, however.

Activity 2
Reflect on Your Faith

Goal: To discuss the importance of being open to God's word and will

Materials: Bibles, newsprint, markers

Read aloud the parable of the sower, also known as the parable of the seed, in Matthew 13:1–9, 18–23. Pause for a moment or two for quiet reflection, and then read it aloud again. Ask the group to listen rather than follow in their Bibles during these readings.

On newsprint, list the four places the seeds landed as named in the parable. Print them across the page or leave space under each one. Although the group will probably be able to recall these places without looking at the printed word, they may want to refer to Matthew during this discussion to have a clear idea of the context for each one.

Looking at the places listed on the newsprint one at a time, have the group suggest what stifles the growth of the seed and then how that image helps them understand what impedes

our hearing of God's Word. Encourage several interpretations rather than focusing on a single idea.

Finally, read the quote from Douglas R. A. Hare found on page 25 in chapter 3.

Discuss the implications of this way of interpreting the parable. How does it mesh with the group's understanding of the connection between commitments and faith, between faith and daily living, and with their mission statement?

For groups of families

Materials: Bible

Read aloud the parable of the sower, Matthew 13:1–9. Form four groups, of any size. One group will be the path and birds; another, the rocky road; a third, the bed of thorns; and the fourth, the good soil. Select one person to be the sower. Have the groups decide how they will portray their assignment. Read the parable again, asking the groups to portray what they do to the seeds as the sower broadcasts seeds on each one as it is named and described in the parable.

Conclude this activity by talking together about the "good soil" we need to be, in order to hear and act on God's word. Make this discussion concrete so the children will move away from the soil metaphor to thinking about their own faithfulness. Young people and adults will make that transition more easily. If there is time, each family might reflect on how their mission statement encourages them to be "good soil."

For groups of parents

Materials: Bible

One task of Christian parents is to nurture their children in the faith. While this is a task for which the congregation promises support, parents are on the front line every day. Thus, one factor in how they determine the balance among personal and family, work, and church responsibilities is how that balance helps them work at this nurturing task.

Read the parable of the sower from Matthew two times, as described in the basic activity. After a general discussion of possible interpretations of the four places that the seeds land, focus the conversation on the parental task of nurturing their children in the faith. How does each place named in the parable correspond to the lives of children and families? What produces the "good soil" needed for the faith of children to grow and mature? How have they included this important nurturing in their family mission statement?

In retreat settings

Materials: Bible, writing paper, pens

Read the parable twice. Explore the meaning of the four places the seeds landed as described in the basic activity above. Then ask small groups to rewrite the parable using contemporary settings of their own choosing. When the groups are ready, ask them to read or act out their parables.

Activity 3
Enter the Focus Question

Goal: To select an area of desired change in the balancing of personal and family, work, and church responsibilities

Materials: individuals' lists and other work from previous sessions, writing paper, pens (optional: recording of quiet instrumental music and player)

In the previous session, the participants have determined the commitments that are most important to them and have pondered some implications for their lives if these values are lived out. Now they are at the point of determining what changes in their lives would help them live their commitments more fully or live more faithfully as children of God, disciples of Jesus Christ. For this activity, the participants will need the lists of commitments they made in Session 1 and any other notes or papers, such as the daily schedules, that will help them determine changes that will produce good or better soil for living faithful lives.

After everyone has the necessary papers and additional writing paper, explain that now they are ready to select one way they can change their lives so that the balance of the major responsibilities they have will lead them to more faithful living. They are to look over their lists of faith values and other papers, ponder what they know about themselves, and determine one change they wish to make in the next two to three weeks. A question to help them begin might be: What is one thing I or my family could do to live more faithfully? Suggest that they start not with a big or dramatic change, but with one that will be significant but manageable. Success breeds success. Once they have accomplished one change, they can look to another possibility.

Provide quiet time for the participants to work individually. During this time, you may play quiet instrumental music, such as recordings by George Winston or Paul Winter.

For groups of families

Materials: family shields, family mission statements, family lists of potential changes

Ask each family to sit in a circle. Introduce the task as selecting a change for their family that will move them closer to fulfilling their mission statement. Begin this process with a time of prayer and silence. Then ask each family member to name one desired change. However, before the second person speaks, he or she must repeat what the previous person said to that person's satisfaction. This simple communication technique, once learned, can be used at other times by the family. It is particularly good when two strong opinions collide. This technique slows the conversation down, includes each family member, and allows time for thinking to occur.

After everyone has contributed, they can discuss the suggestions and come to a consensus on one they are willing to try. This change may be one suggested by a family member, a variation of a suggestion, or an idea that grew out of their discussion.

For groups of parents

Materials: individuals' lists and other work from previous sessions, writing paper, pens (optional: recording of quiet instrumental music and player)

Groups of parents might proceed as in the basic activity above. However, as they select their area of change, suggest that they consider this question: What will help me function better as a parent, as one responsible for nurturing the faith of my child? Note that the change may or may not be closely tied to a parenting task. Rather, they might look for a change that will add nutrients to the soil needed to nurture their children, borrowing from the metaphor in the parable of the sower. They will begin, of course, with the list of possible changes they made after the previous session.

In retreat settings

Materials: individuals' lists and other work from previous sessions, writing paper, pens

Proceed as above, but extend the reflection time. Suggest that the participants go off on their own and then each find a partner with whom they can check out their ideas. Ideally, these pairs of partners will continue to share ideas and to support and encourage each other following the retreat.

Activity 4
Prepare for Change

Goal: To name the key players in the desired change and plan how to solicit their support

Materials: overhead projector, "Ripples" transparency, plain paper, pencils

Project the transparency, "Ripples." Point out that what happens when an object is dropped into a pool of water is similar to what happens when we change some part of our life or routine. Few changes make an impression only at the initial point. Perhaps you agree to teach a church school class. What ripples would move out from that decision? To your family or those with whom you live? Your friends? Your work? What else? A change will be accomplished more smoothly if we can think in advance about who and what will be affected by it. Then we can explain our decision or alert those persons to the change.

Distribute plain paper and pencils to the group. Ask them to write their desired change in the center of the paper. Then ask them to list where the ripples will be. Who are the key players in those ripples? What do you need to say to them? How might you prepare them for the change as it affects them?

Assign chapter 3 as the reading.

For groups of families

Materials: large sheets of drawing paper or construction paper (light colors), markers (several colors)

The focus for the family in this activity is on how the selected change will affect each family member and what each one must do to help the family accomplish this change. For example, if the change is that they will attend worship together regularly (maybe even every Sunday), what must each family member do to make that happen?

Give each family a large sheet of drawing paper or light-colored construction paper and several colors of markers. Ask each family to choose one family member to print his or her selected change in the middle of the paper. Then ask the family to decide the role each one must play to implement this change, and write those commitments around the edges of the paper, signed by each member. They can post this commitment at home, where they will be reminded of each one's role and the importance of cooperating to accomplish this change.

Ask the parents to read chapter 3.

For groups of parents

Materials: writing paper, pens

Ask each parent to read silently the change (or one of them) she or he selected, but with their child in mind. Ask, "How will this change affect that child? How would that child describe the change and what it means to you?" Ask the parents to write this down, or have them discuss this with a partner in the group.

Their assignment is to read chapter 3.

In retreat settings

In addition to the basic activity above, the retreat setting may provide time to try out some ways to communicate through role plays. Using the descriptions below or others that you devise, ask the participants to role-play the scenes, trying to imagine what would happen and how the person desiring the change might best communicate what is desired and why.

Role Play A. Ralph must convince his father that he can no longer drive safely. His father has driven for more than fifty years and has not had an accident. However, Ralph is aware that his father's judgment is failing, and there are probably other health issues. How might Ralph broach this subject with his father? What might he expect from his father? Where are the ripples in this situation? Who else might be brought into this role play?

Role Play B. Sarah and Joe have agreed that they want to spend more time with their children, Mike (4) and Joe Jr. (7). Now they are working out a plan to do that. Sarah works part-time as a nurse (three nights a week and Saturday morning). Joe works Monday through Friday (8:30–4:30). How might their conversation proceed? How might they divide the care of the children and household tasks?

Role Play C. Marie adopted a baby from another country, who is now three years old. Marie works full-time. In talking with a church member at the social hour, she commented that she would like for her child to have more interactions with adults at the church. The church member has thought about Marie's statement. Now she is on the phone with Marie. How might their conversation go? What creative possibilities might they imagine together?

Role Play D. George is single, but has agreed to spend time with a young boy who is fatherless. His boss, however, appears to assume that George can travel for his job at the drop of a hat. He has just asked George to leave the following day for a three-day trip. George has already promised to take his young friend to a ball game the night after next. How will George handle this request from his boss?

Following each role play, discuss the options presented in it. Then ask, "What else could have happened? What other avenues are there to resolve the issue?"

Activity 5
Nurture Your Spiritual Life

Goal: To pray for others and ourselves

Materials: photocopies of "Intercessory Prayer" (page 89)

Introduce the prayer by reminding the group that alone we will make little headway in changing our lives. Even if we begin, we may become discouraged. An important component in nurturing our spiritual lives is prayer, for others as well as for ourselves.

Distribute the copies of "Intercessory Prayer." Explain that after each petition, there will be a time for silent prayer. Ask everyone to pray the concluding section aloud in unison.

For group of families

Materials: photocopies of "Intercessory Prayer" (page 89)

Ask two or three families to come together to form small groups. Explain that they are welcome to pray aloud or silently as directed during the prayer. Take care to allow enough time for all who wish to pray aloud before praying the next part of the prayer aloud.

For groups of parents

Materials: photocopies of "Intercessory Prayer" (page 89)

Proceed with the intercessory prayer as in the basic activity above.

In retreat settings

Materials: photocopies of "Intercessory Prayer" (page 89)

Distribute the copies of the intercessory prayer. Suggest that they use this prayer as a guide for a time of personal prayer and meditation. Also pray this prayer together at the close of the program today or at the end of the retreat.

Additional Activity: Practice Communication Skills

To rehearse how to communicate effectively, use this activity during extra time in a retreat schedule, in an additional session before Session 4, or as a meeting after a few months.

Read about the role of communication in chapter 3. Use that information to help introduce this activity, particularly noting the importance of speaking clearly and listening carefully. Select from these activities:

—Form groups of three or four persons. Ask one person to go outside the space to examine a geometric illustration that you have drawn earlier (combine a square, a rectangle, a circle, and a straight line in any way you wish). Give each remaining person a sheet of paper and a pencil. Ask them to listen to the person's description of the illustration and, without helping one another, draw it on the paper. The describer can use only words, no gestures, and cannot make any comment about anyone's drawing. The describer can return to look at the illustration again, if necessary. When you have used up the time allotted or when some people believe they have correctly followed the directions given them, bring the illustration to the group. Talk with them about the process and the place words played in it.

—Print these sentences, or others you think of, on newsprint or a chalkboard:

Everybody wants something from me.

I feel guilty (working, volunteering, staying home).

Nobody in this house helps me.

I have no time to myself.

My (mom, dad) is never home.

I have to do all the jobs nobody else wants.

Form pairs of participants. Ask one person to select a sentence and think about how to say it. Then the person says it to the partner, and the two converse.

The role of the partner is to listen carefully to what the first person says and to help that person clarify her or his position. Of course, the first person should be listening carefully as well.

Stop the conversations when they are still in full swing. Talk together about the difficulty of listening, especially when you have an investment in what is being said.

—Use the listening exercise for families in "Enter the Focus Question." This works well with all ages.

Intercessory Prayer

God of all time, of all choices, and of all changes, meet us now in this time that we have set apart to speak our prayers to you. Open our hearts to your word even as we seek your heart for our words.

We pray for those who live each day without the knowledge of your love and care.

(silence)

We pray for those who earnestly seek a life that is worthy of your calling.

(silence)

We pray for children, young people, and adults who struggle to live faithfully.

(silence)

We pray for those who search for change and must convince others of its importance.

(silence)

We pray even for ourselves, knowing that you desire our prayers.

(silence)

God of all our lives, stay with us. Watch over us. Make your presence known to us and grant us peace. In Jesus' name. Amen.

Ripples

The pebble creates ripples far beyond where it entered the water.

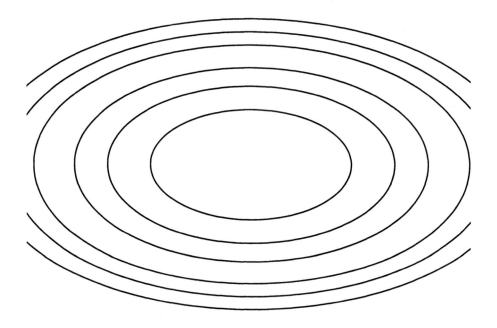

Permission is granted for the leader to copy this page for distribution to the participants for use as an overhead transparency.

Session Four
Creative Problem Solving

Focus question: What can I do about the obstacles that appear when I institute a change?

No matter how carefully you plan ahead for the ripples that the smallest change will produce, surprises always crop up. Since one change automatically alters related parts of your life, life is more a series of changes than a static existence. Viewing change as a way of life and looking for ways to work creatively with these obstacles related to change is an important part of daily life.

In this session, the participants will examine their attitude toward change in general and try some creative problem-solving techniques.

Session Outline (60 minutes)

1. Introduce This Session
   5–10 minutes

2. Reflect on Your Faith
   15 minutes

3. Enter the Focus Question
   5–10 minutes

4. Examine Your Life
   20 minutes

5. Nurture Your Spiritual Life
   10 minutes

To Prepare for This Session

—Photocopy "Some Serious and Not-So-Serious Questions to Ask When Solving a Problem Created by a Change (page 104)," one for each participant.
—Duplicate the transparency "Change is like . . ." (page 103).
—Meditate on Psalm 131.

Activity 1
Introduce This Session

Goal: To review the main points of the previous sessions and to gather comments and questions from the participants

Materials: overhead projector; transparencies for Sessions 1, 2, and 3

Display the overhead transparencies for the first three sessions. As you show each one, have the group recall the use of the transparency in that session and other main points from the session.

Also allow time for the group members to tell of their experiences with establishing the desired change. How did it go? Was it easier or more difficult than they expected? Refrain from moving into the area of how the change may have affected others and other parts of one's life, which will be covered in Activity 3.

For groups of families

Materials: overhead projector, transparencies for Sessions 1, 2, and 3

Ask each family to sit together. Display the transparencies one at a time, allowing time for the family groups to talk among themselves. Ask them to identify something that they connect with each transparency by completing this sentence: "This picture reminds me . . ." Have them go around their circle at least two times.

Bring everyone together and hear some of the ideas that they recalled.

For groups of parents

Materials: transparencies for Sessions 1, 2, and 3

Review by recalling the focus question for each previous session. Form three groups, and assign one question to each group. Ask them to talk together about the main points covered in the book or in the session for that question. Ask each small group to report to the large group, presenting the major points from that session in two to four sentences. Provide each group with the appropriate transparency as a focal point for their summary.

In retreat settings

Materials: posters with main points from Sessions 1, 2, and 3; colored markers

Continue to post the main points from the session. Set out colored markers and encourage participants to add their own ideas, thoughts, and questions to each one. Illustrations as well as words are appropriate.

Activity 2
Reflect on Your Faith

Goal: To recall that God works in many ways to help us be the creative beings that we are meant to be

Materials: Bibles

In both the Old and New Testaments of the Bible, we read of God's surprises. God tells Moses, a man with a speech difficulty, to go to the Pharaoh and plead for the release of the Israelites from their Egyptian slavery. God sends a messiah, a Jew born in the stable, to be savior of the world. This Jesus the Christ eats with outcasts and talks with, even teaches, women. He blesses children and heals young and old. Yet even Jesus was brought up short by a Syrophoenician woman seeking healing for her daughter.

Read Mark 7:24–30 aloud. Ask the group to close their eyes and imagine the story as you read it again. Suggest that they open their eyes and follow the story in their Bibles as you or another group member reads the story a third time. This time, ask them to listen to the story in light of the topic for this session, creative problem solving. How did the woman approach her problem? What ripples did her approach make? What happened to Jesus? What was his understanding of his work at the beginning of the passage? How did it change? What prompted the change? What were the surprises in the story? How may this incident have changed the rest of Jesus' ministry?

For groups of families

Materials: Bible, woman, young girl

Listen to the story as told by the Syrophoenician woman. Invite a woman and young girl to portray the mother and her daughter. The mother will tell the story to the group. Her daughter might be seated on her lap. A sample story is on page 100. The daughter might describe her amazement at being healed suddenly. Explain that the story is found in the Gospels of Matthew and Mark. Talk together about the ways that the woman, her daughter, and Jesus must have been changed by this incident.

For groups of parents

Materials: Bible

Read and discuss the story as described in the basic activity above. During the last reading have the group listen to the story specifically as parents. Ponder what might have brought the woman, a Gentile, to seek out Jesus, especially since the text is clear that he came to this place to remove himself from the crowds. What would cause her to act so brashly?

In retreat settings

Materials: Bibles, copies of "Lectio Divina" (page 101)

Take more time with Mark 7:24–30 by having the participants read it individually, using the process described on page 101 known as *lectio divina*.

Activity 3
Enter the Focus Question

Goal: To consider the ways your desired change affected other persons and other areas of your life

Materials: overhead projector, "Change is like . . ." transparency (page 103), plain paper, pens or pencils

Show the group the transparency, "Change is like . . ." Talk together about the effect of one small change on persons important in one's life and work. Review the examples in chapter 4. Then give each group member a sheet of plain paper and a pen or pencil. Ask them to print the change they instituted in the middle of the page. Around it ask them to write the "sparks" that were ignited by this change. When they have finished, ask each person to find a partner; ask the pairs to question each other to see if there are any sparks that they missed.

For groups of families

Materials: large sheets of paper, copies of the diagram

Give each family a large sheet of paper and a copy of the diagram below:

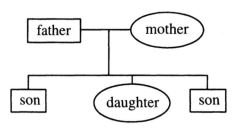

Instruct them to draw a diagram of their own family using this method. Males are boxes; females are circles. Then at the top of the page print the change that they are trying. Below

each person on the family diagram, write how the change has affected that person. Allow each family member time to speak, rather than having the family determine how it has affected each member. Remind them that how a family member thinks he or she is affected is as important as how others in the family think that member was affected. Stop them at this point. Looking for solutions comes in Activity 4.

For groups of parents

Materials: writing paper, pencils

Provide writing paper and pencils. Have each person work alone to make a list of the ways the change affected others—family members, employers and employees, neighbors, friends. When they have finished, they can compare their lists with one or two other persons. This comparison may open up new avenues for them.

In retreat settings

Select one or more of the situations below for the group to discuss. Or invite them to devise their own situations, based on the types of changes they are considering. Since they are in a retreat setting, they probably cannot begin to implement the changes they have identified. This type of activity can help them anticipate what happens when a change is introduced.

—Annie decided a change important for her was to establish a quiet, meditative time. She chose to get up fifteen minutes earlier to read a psalm and pray. The first morning her husband grumbled when the alarm went off. The second morning her three-year-old daughter woke up and wanted breakfast. What can Annie do?

—George proposed a new family schedule for Saturdays. He wanted everyone to pitch in on the weekend chores in the morning. Then everyone would be free to do what they wanted in the afternoon, but they would have dinner together and spend the evening together. His wife is lukewarm to the idea, his teenage son is close to belligerent, and his ten-year-old son thinks it would be good. What can George do?

—Maria's mother lives with Maria and her family (husband and three teenage children). The grandmother has begun to forget things, from where she left her glasses to turning off the stove after she cooks. Grandmother is alone three mornings a week when Maria teaches in a preschool program. What can this family do?

Activity 4
Examine Your Life

Goal: To look creatively at a myriad of ways to solve problems

Materials: newsprint, marker, photocopies of "Some Serious and Not-So-Serious Questions to Ask

When Solving a Problem Created by a Change" (page 102)

Ask for a volunteer to present a problem for the group to think about. The volunteer will probably need to state the desired change and then explain briefly what resulted. Then, ask the volunteer to listen as the group ponders the difficulty and ways to approach it. Remind them to turn off "the judge" in their minds. Their task is to provide as many ways as they can to work with the difficulty. Nothing, short of harming another person, is off-limits. One person, or a leader, should write all their ideas on newsprint so the group can build on what has already been said. When they have run out of steam, distribute the copies of "Some Serious and Not-So-Serious Questions to Ask When Solving a Problem Created by a Change." Try a few of the questions there to see if more ideas surface.

This can also be done in groups of five to seven people so more individuals have an opportunity for this kind of help.

Assign chapter 4 as the reading for the next session.

For groups of families

Materials: large shoe boxes or cardboard cartons, paint and brush or construction paper and glue, hole punch, strip of cloth, photocopies of "Some Serious and Not-So-Serious Questions to Ask When Solving a Problem Created by a Change" (page 102)

For each two families, make a shoe from a large shoebox or cardboard carton. Paint the box or cover the sides of the box with paper. Punch holes for shoelaces in the sides. Thread a strip of cloth, bright or somber, through the holes like shoelaces.

Ask each family to join another family. Begin with a difficulty created by the change for one of the families. Ask the other family to think of as many ways as they can to help the situation. However, a person can talk only when she or he is wearing the shoe. After all, you don't know what another person's life is like unless you walk in her or his shoes. So the shoes are a reminder not to judge what is being said or what has already been done.

Appoint one person of the family presenting the difficulty to be the scribe. She or he is to write down all the suggestions, so the family will have them to consider at another time.

Allot the time so each family will have a time to gather suggestions. If there is a lull in the ideas, distribute "Some Serious and Not-So-Serious Questions to Ask When Solving a Problem Created by a Change." Otherwise, distribute it to each family at the end of the session.

Ask the adults to read chapter 4 before the next session.

For groups of parents

Materials: newsprint, markers, photocopies of "Some Serious and Not-So-Serious Questions to Ask When Solving a Problem Created by a Change" (page 102)

Give the group members a few minutes to look over the previous activity and think about both the positive effects and the difficulties that this change has instigated. Ask two or three persons to describe the change they instituted and the difficulties they are now encountering. Do this one at a time. After each one, brainstorm actions to counter the most serious difficulties. Brainstorming does not include evaluation of any idea, either by the group or the person who presented the description. To liven the brainstorming, give them a question or two from "Some Serious and Not-So-Serious Questions to Ask When Solving a Problem Created by a Change." Distribute copies of this page at the end of the session. Instead, or if there is not enough time, you might give the list to the person to ponder alone or with persons of his or her choice at another time.

Assign chapter 4 as homework.

In retreat settings

Materials: foam blocks or modeling clay, florist wire or pipe cleaners, index cards, colored markers, scissors

Create stabiles, each of which focuses on a single change and its effects on others. A stabile is a group of objects mounted on wires that are affixed to a solid base. If the retreat group includes families, each one might work as a team. Another way to organize the teams is by the subject matter of the proposed change.

Provide a base for the stabile, such

as a foam block or a large lump of modeling clay. Provide florist wire or pipe cleaners. Set out a stack of index cards, (several colors, if possible), colored markers, and scissors. On the index cards, which can be cut into all kinds of interesting shapes, the artists can print their ideas for solving the problem they chose. The shapes are then attached to the pipe cleaners or pieces of florist wire and stuck into the base in an arrangement pleasing to the eyes of the creators. Print the problem on a large card, and place it in front of the stabile.

All ages can engage in this project.

Activity 5
Nurture Your Spiritual Life

Goal: To pray the Psalms

Materials: Bibles, recording of soft instrumental music and player

The Psalms of the Hebrew Scriptures provide us with words to express our emotions. When we are familiar with the variety of feelings expressed by the psalmists, we can go to this book whenever we are at a loss for words to speak to God, or to create a place and time where God may speak to us.

Important to holding on to a change in the midst of it is the knowledge of God's presence and trust. This trust is frequently the closing thought of a psalm of despair, such as Psalm 131.

Have the group members sit comfortably in a chair, with their feet flat on the floor and their hands relaxed in their lap. Invite them to close their eyes as you play soft instrumental

music for a minute or two. Suggest that they relax each part of their body, beginning with their toes, as they listen to the music. Turn the music down slowly. Then read, slowly and gently, Psalm 131. Repeat the last verse three or four times, pausing after each reading. Then turn the music up slowly until it is at the level it was earlier and invite the participants to open their eyes when they are ready.

For groups of families

Materials: photocopies of "If You Will Only Let God Guide You" (optional: piano) (page 99)

Distribute the photocopies of "If You Will Only Let God Guide You." Since this hymn may be new to some members of the group, take time to read it before singing it and talk about the words. Remind the children, young people, and adults that remembering that we can trust in God will often help us get through difficult times. Then sing the hymn together.

For groups of parents

Materials: Bible, recording of soft instrumental music and player

Begin by inviting the participants to prepare for the meditation as in the basic activity above, but ask them to picture in their minds each of their children before you begin to read Psalm 131. Suggest that they imagine their children standing by them, perhaps with a hand on their shoulders. Then proceed as described above.

In retreat settings

Materials: photocopies of "If You Will Only Let God Guide You" (page 99) (optional: piano)

Since this activity will probably come at the end of the evening program, place it in the format of a closing time of worship. Read Psalm 131. Pray, allowing a time for sentence prayers from anyone in the group. Sing "If You Will Only Let God Guide You."

"If You Will Only Let God Guide You"

If You Will Only Let God Guide You

Georg Neumark, 1667
Tr. by Catherine Winkworth, 1827-1878
Altered, 1972

NEUMARK 9.8.9.8.8.8.
Melody by George Neumark, 1667

Moderately ♩=96

If you will on - ly let God guide you, And hope in God through

all your ways, What - ev - er comes, God stands be - side you

And sees you through the hard - est days, O trust in God's un -

chang - ing love; Build on the Rock that can - not move.

Permission is granted for the leader to copy this page for distribution to the participants in the group.

Mark 7:24–30,
as told by the Syrophoenician woman

My daughter is very precious to me. I delight in her as much as I delight in my sons, perhaps more.

When an unclean spirit entered her, I was crushed. I tried everything that my friends suggested. I cannot begin to tell you all the things I did. Nothing worked. Finally, I was without hope.

Then, a few days ago, the women at the well were talking about a Jewish teacher who was in the area. We were all surprised that he would come here, to this land despised by the Jews. Some had heard about this man named Jesus, who is also a healer. I listened to their stories, but I did not tell them what was in my head.

On the way home, I determined my plan. I did not tell anyone, not even my family, what I was going to do.

I listened carefully whenever anyone spoke of Jesus until I was sure where this teacher and healer was staying in our village. Then, still telling no one where I was going, I went to the house where he had been seen.

When I saw him, I knelt at his feet and bowed my head to the floor. "Please, please," I begged, "cast the unclean spirit from my daughter."

I was shocked when I heard him say, "Let the children be fed first, for it is not fair to give the children's food to the dogs." Was he saying that the children of Israel were better and more important than we Gentiles? He wasn't even looking at me.

In my concern for my daughter, I spoke without thinking, "Sir, even the dogs under the table eat the children's crumbs."

Jesus was startled. He looked right at me and said, "For saying that, you may go. The unclean spirit has left your daughter."

I left quickly. When I got home, I hurried to my daughter's bed. There she was, sleeping peacefully. The unclean spirit was gone!

To this day, I remember Jesus' face when he looked at me. I will never forget him.

Lectio Divina

—Read the text aloud twice. The second time read it slowly, listening for a word or phrase that seems to capture your imagination. Ponder that word or phrase for a time, saying it quietly to yourself over and over.

—Read the passage again. This time watch or listen for the feeling that is attached to the word or phrase identified in the previous readings.

—Read the passage once more. Then ponder how the word or phrase and its attached feelings are connected with you, your time and place, your concerns or joys. Sit for quite some time, silently, in God's presence.

—When you are ready, stand and give thanks to God.

Some Serious and Not-So-Serious Questions to Ask When Solving a Problem Created by a Change

—What is the obvious or "right" answer?

—What is the less obvious or next "right" answer?

—What kind of animal is this problem like?

—What do you feed that animal or problem to make it feel good?

—How would you solve this problem if it were upside-down?

—What is the key word or phrase in the problem?

—How can you use that key word or phrase in restating the problem? In naming a solution?

—What metaphor or symbol is hidden in the problem statement?

—How might this metaphor be used to solve the problem? Think of at least three ways to do this.

—What spoken or unspoken rules are attached to this problem?

—Which rules are really necessary? Which ones can be tossed out?

—What "what if" questions can you ask about this problem?

—Consider each person affected by this problem. How would each one complete this sentence: "The best thing to do about this problem is . . ."

—If this problem were a cartoon, what would it be?

—What is the weirdest solution that you can think of for this problem?

—Go around the circle at least four times for everyone to complete this sentence: "If I had this problem, I would . . ."

Change

Change is like fireworks: One spark and a thousand new lights sparkle above you.

Session Five
Keep On Keeping On

*Focus question: Where can I find support
to keep at these changes?*

This final session helps the participants summarize what they have learned and experienced. Just as importantly, it points toward paths that will help them maintain their desired changes and give them a continued focus on their faith.

Be ready with suggestions for follow-up meetings and other ways the group and individuals can find support as they struggle with change. An important part of making these changes is recognizing that such changes are often against the flow of the primary culture. Not for the first time, the church needs to stand outside and over against the society in which it exists. However, we in North America have not often found ourselves in such a stance.

You will probably want to include a way for the group to evaluate this course and its effectiveness for participants, as well as the process. See the next page for evaluation helps. They can be inserted into the session whenever it seems to fit most appropriately for your group.

Session Outline (60 minutes)

1. Review the Previous Sessions
   5–10 minutes

2. Reflect on Your Faith
   15 minutes

3. Enter the Focus Question
   5–10 minutes

4. Plan for Your Life after This Course
   20 minutes

5. Nurture Your Spiritual Life
   10 minutes

To Prepare for This Session

—Select a method for the evaluation by the participants, and prepare any necessary materials.
—Pray the "Litany" that will be given to the participants.

Methods for Participant Evaluation

—Graffiti sheets: Tape three sheets of newsprint to a wall or to a table. Label them: "Some of the best things about this course," "Something that might be changed about this course," and "Something else I want to say." Provide markers of different colors for the participants to write their ideas and suggestions on the appropriate newsprint sheets.
—Immediate thoughts: This method is sometimes called "popcorn" evaluation because it pops up all over the group. Because it is so immediate, the comments often build on what has just been said. Read an incomplete sentence from the list below or create your own. The participants are to complete the sentence, speaking in no particular order, and they can speak more than once. If yours is a talkative group, set a timer for a minute or so for each sentence.

"This course was like . . ."

"My favorite moment in the course was . . ."

"I will never again . . ."

"The spiritual disciplines were . . ."

"The Bible study was . . ."

"Reading the participant's chapters . . ."

"What I need now is . . ."

"Throughout these sessions I . . ."

To keep track of the comments, record this segment on a cassette, or have one or two persons act as scribes.

—Formal evaluation: Distribute copies of the handout, "Course Evaluation." Provide time for the participants to complete them before they leave.

Activity 1
Review the Previous Sessions

Goal: To review the highlights of the course

Materials: overhead projector and the transparencies for Sessions 1, 2, 3, and 4

Forms groups of three or four persons. Show the transparencies from each session, one at a time, allowing each one to remain on the screen for at least two minutes. Begin with the transparency for Session 4, "Change Is Like . . ." and continue back to the one for Session 1, "Symbol." The groups are to recall important points from each session, saying them aloud.

Keep the pace moving. If a group draws a blank, show the transparency again at the end of the sequence so others can help them recall the highlights of that session.

Before moving to the next activity, invite questions or comments from the group about the previous sessions or about their experiences as they work on change.

For groups of families

Materials: overhead projector, transparencies for Sessions 1, 2, 3, and 4

Have each family group sit together and form a circle. Project the transparency for Session 1. Give each family group a couple minutes to create one sentence that they want to tell someone else about what happened in that session. Call time. Invite one family member from each group go to the next group clockwise. When the person has delivered the message, she or he returns to the family.

Review each session in the same way. A different family member should take the message each time, repeating persons only if there are not enough family members. For each message, have them go to a different

family group. For example, the message from Session 2 can be taken to the group next to them counter-clockwise. For Session 3, they might go to the group directly across from them, and for Session 4, to the second group clockwise around the room.

Conclude by having one person from each family group tell something about how they are progressing on their desired change.

For groups of parents

Materials: overhead projector, transparencies for Sessions 1, 2, 3, and 4

Show the transparencies for the previous sessions, changing each one after thirty seconds. Invite the group during the time the transparency is shown to call out anything that they recall as important about that session. The group may need a couple tries to warm up to this activity. Keep showing the transparencies in the same order, recycling them three or four times as the group members call out their memories.

Allow time for the group to ask questions of one another about how their desired change is working. During conversations such as this, they will discover those persons with whom they have a particular resonance and who might be good support partners for them in the coming weeks and months.

In retreat settings

Materials: posters with the main points from Sessions 1, 2, 3, and 4; markers

Take a few minutes for persons to add comments to the posters. Then read what others have written, without comment. Suggest that the posters will be up until the end of the retreat, if there are comments they still wish to make. Save the posters as a part of the evaluation and for any ideas that they contain about future programming.

Activity 2
Reflect on Your Faith

Goal: To ponder how your faith can help you keep all things in perspective

Materials: Bibles, newsprint, marker

Introduce the Scripture with the following points:
—Living in such a way that one's personal, work, and church responsibilities are balanced will often put us at odds with the rest of society.
—In the Scripture passage for this session, it is clear that a problem has erupted in the church at Colossae, but we do not know from the letter just what it is.
—The goal of this passage is "perfect harmony."

Ask that the group listen for the attributes that are needed to live the new life in Christ. Provide Bibles for those who wish to read along. However, some people find it easier to listen when they are not looking at the printed word. Read Colossians 3:9–17 aloud.

Following the reading, ask, "What attributes did you hear?" Print their answers on newsprint. Then discuss together the communal nature of this passage. The letter assumes a group of believers. How does that assumption make a difference in your hearing and understanding of these words? How does being centered in your faith give you a different perspective on what brings "perfect harmony?"

For groups of families

Materials: shelf paper or banner paper, scissors, Bibles, colored papers, markers, glue

In advance, cut accordion chains of people from plain shelf paper or banner paper. The bigger the figures, the more fun to work with them.

Read Colossians 3:9–17 aloud to the entire group. Then give each family enough people in a chain to represent each family member. Have them clothe the persons with the attributes named in the passage. Provide a variety of colored papers, markers, and glue to each family. Once they have clothed the figures with paper, they can print the attributes on the pieces of clothing.

For groups of parents

Materials: Bibles, index cards, markers, fabric, large safety pins

Read Colossians 3:9–17 aloud. Take a few minutes to discuss the passage, using the questions above. Then give each person an index card and a marker. Ask them to print on the index cards the attribute(s) they feel they most need as parents who juggle their various responsibilities. Then give each person a large safety pin and a swatch of fabric large enough to cover the index card. They can pin the card with the fabric over it to their clothing.

In retreat settings

Materials: Bibles, fabric or crepe paper strips, felt or construction paper, scissors, markers, glue

After reading and discussing the passage from Colossians, provide all participants with strips of a sturdy fabric or crepe paper, 4 inches by 5 feet for adults and shorter strips for children. Ask them to cut hearts from felt or construction paper, write on the hearts the attributes named in Colossians 3:9–17, and glue the hearts to the fabric or paper strip, in any order desired. They are creating stoles that can clothe them with love and be a reminder of this passage after leaving the retreat.

Activity 3
Enter the Focus Question

Goal: To acknowledge what support you have already found

Introduce this activity by reading the focus question: Where can I find support to keep at these changes? Then point out that one source of support is what we learn from studying and reading the Bible. Ask the group to recall the kinds of helpful and supportive learnings they have gleaned from this course.

Then ask them to identify other sources of support that they have experienced from this course. Some may name the spiritual disciplines included in each session; others may think immediately of group members who have become a source of strength and support for them. Affirm their ideas.

For groups of families

Families need to recognize how they support one another and, thus, the family as a whole. Invite each family member to take a turn standing or sitting in the middle of the family circle as the other family members take turns naming qualities and skills of the person in the middle that help the family work together or add to family life in some other positive way.

For groups of parents

Materials: newsprint and marker or chalkboard and chalk, writing paper, pencils

Through this activity, the participants can begin to identify, for themselves, those persons who have been most helpful during this course. Print the following list in a row on newsprint or a chalkboard where everyone will be able to see it: asks good questions, says comforting words, is a calming presence, motivates me to action, listens carefully, sees many points of view, makes me laugh.

Give each person a sheet of paper and a pencil. Have them print those items on their paper that they feel they most often need from others. Then next to each one, print the name of someone in the group who performs that deed.

After they have exhausted the names of group members, ask them to add friends and family members who provide these kinds of support.

This list need not be shown to others, but it will used in Activity 5 by each person.

In retreat settings

Materials: writing paper, pencils, list of participants with addresses and phone numbers

If the retreat group is made up entirely of adults, they can make the list as suggested for the groups of parents above. If the group did not know one another when they arrived, this may be more difficult for them. However, they have probably each found one or two persons with whom they feel comfortable in conversation.

If the retreat group includes families, they might do the activity suggested for groups of families. Or they may also make a list of persons from the retreat they want to see when they get home. If the retreat group is from a wide area or more than one congregation, see that a list of names and addresses with e-mail addresses is given to each person.

Activity 4
Plan for Your Life
after This Course

Goal: To become aware of ways to find the necessary support outside this course

Materials: newsprint and marker or chalkboard and chalk

Some ideas about how the group can support one another, now that this course is ending, may have surfaced in the previous activities. Name them now and list them on newsprint or a chalkboard. Then invite other ideas from the group.

If there is a desire to gather again after two or three months, set a date, time, and place now. Although the participants may not know their schedules that far in advance, it is easier to attempt this with everyone present than to do it at a later date. If the selection of a date is not possible, try to pinpoint several tentative dates. Ask for a volunteer to poll the group after this session to get the dates possible for each one. This can be done by phone, e-mail, or letter. Set the date as soon as possible so it can be placed on everyone's calendar.

Ask what they would like to happen at that meeting. The group should take charge of its group life, rather than relying on a leader from this course. Encourage two or three participants to share this responsibility, if necessary.

Look over the suggestions the group named earlier to see if there are likely ideas for your group.

For groups of families

As much as family members can help one another, every family also needs support from other persons. That help may come from many sources: friends at school or work, other family members, friends at church. In advance, recruit a few group members (up to four or five) to meet with you to organize some extended family groups. Invite persons who are particularly skilled at noticing the social nuances of friendships and persons who gravitate to each other. Organize extended families by putting together three or four families who have some things in common, such as ages of children, similar hobbies, sports interests, or a common heritage.

Announce the extended families that you have organized. Have those groups gather and decide on something they can do together. At that time they can also check on how they are progressing in their desired changes. They may meet for a potluck supper or a picnic. Or they may go for a hike together, stopping to talk together at a special spot along the way. What they plan is limited only by their imaginations. Suggest that they start with something simple, however, and that they find a time when everyone can be present.

For groups of parents

Parents with children of the same age or those with similar backgrounds usually find one another in a course of this length. However, they may need a little help to figure out ways to keep in touch after this last session. The process you choose will depend upon how well acquainted the participants are and how large the group is. Here are some ideas to help that to happen:

—Suggest that the parents with children of similar ages meet together. They can discuss ways they might stay in touch—anything from a monthly social time with children included to gathering for dessert periodically when the children are not present.

—Plan a "reunion" once a quarter during the time that the children are in church school or some other church program.

—Ask the group to look at the list of the special gifts and skills of the participants they made earlier. Suggest that, before they leave, they contact one person on their list to talk by phone or set up a simple meeting within the next two weeks.

—Appoint a committee of three to plan a reunion for the group in three or four months.

In retreat settings

Materials: writing paper or index cards, pencils

The real test of change comes when the retreat participants return home and actually try to do what they have been discussing and planning. One issue for them will be how to keep the enthusiasm and support that they felt during the retreat when they are no longer with the group.

In advance, have each participant list on a sheet of paper three persons from the group with whom she or he would like to continue contact following the retreat. The leaders can, working with the individual preferences, pair the participants.

Explain that the pairings or buddies are for support in making the changes they have discussed. Some buddies will connect more quickly than others; some may never click at all. Together determine a length of time for the buddies to stay in touch, perhaps three months. After that time, the buddy system is defunct, unless individuals choose to continue the contact.

Activity 5
Nurture Your Spiritual Life

Goal: To conclude the course with a time of dedication and prayer

Materials: overhead projector, "Bear with One Another" transparency (page 115), recording of instrumental music and player, Bible, photocopies of "Litany"

Play music softly as a time of transition from the group discussion and planning to their worship together. Soothing instrumental music is a good choice. Turn it up slowly when you are ready to begin rather than suddenly blasting the room with music. Use the worship ideas here or create your own design. Turn on the overhead projector to show the transparency, "Bear with One Another." Distribute the photocopies of "Litany."
Read Colossians 3:14–17.
Pray the litany.

For groups of families

Materials: overhead projector, "Bear with One Another" transparency (page 115), stoles made earlier, Bible, photocopies of "Litany," (page 113), newsprint and marker

Ask the group members to wear the stoles they made. Follow the same worship design as above.
For the litany, ask for several read-

ers, representing the age groups present. Teach the response to the group before you begin the time of worship. Print it on newsprint for those who can read. The group will know to say it when the reader stops or sits down or by some other signal that you devise.

For groups of parents

Materials: overhead projector, "Bear with One Another" transparency (page 115), recording of instrumental music and player, Bible, photocopies of "Litany" (page 113).

The worship design above or your adaption of it will be fine for groups of parents. Suggest that they pray the litany at home with their children or adapt it to make it appropriate to the ages of their children.

In retreat settings

Materials: overhead projector, "Bear with One Another" transparency (page 115), recording of instrumental music and player, Bible, photocopies of "Litany," (page 113), hymnbooks, paper hearts or index cards, pens

For a retreat setting, this activity will probably be the culminating one for the entire event. Therefore, you may want to expand the design above, including singing and more time for personal dedication. Here are some ideas:

—Sing a hymn of dedication, such as "Take Thou Our Minds, Dear

Lord," "How Clear Is Our Vocation, Lord," "Be Thou My Vision," or "The Voice of God Is Calling."

—Distribute paper hearts or index cards and pens. Invite the participants to write on the heart or card their desired change. When everyone has finished, ask them to tear the paper or heart in half. One half will be gathered as an offering to God; the other half will be taken home as a reminder of their pledge.

—Include some or all of the Bible passages included in this course.

Litany

Leader: Creator God, we come to you who made us in your image.

People: Hear our prayer, O God.

Leader: We have struggled to hear your call, your call to each of us and to all of us. Open our ears to your voice.

People: Hear our prayer, O God.

Leader: We have strained to find our ways, individually and together, to follow the example of Jesus Christ, whom you sent to show us your love. Open our eyes to see him lead us.

People: Hear our prayer, O God.

Leader: We are trying to live in our new selves, the selves that you have given us through Jesus Christ. Open our hearts to accept this wonderful gift.

People: Hear our prayer, O God.

Leader: We seek the strength shown in those saints who have followed where you have led, from Abraham and Sarah to the members of our con-gregation who share their lives and faith with us. Continue to bless us, O God.

People: Hear our prayer, O God.

Leader: Loving God, we each have particular concerns as we work to balance our personal, work, and church responsibilities so that we may lead faithful lives. Hear now our individual prayers as we say them in our hearts.

(pause)

Knowing that God's love always surrounds us and that Christ's example is ever before us, listen to this benediction and take its words of courage and comfort with you:

Go forth into the world in peace; be of good courage; hold fast to that which is good; render no one evil for evil; strengthen the fainthearted; support the weak; help the afflicted; honor all people; love and serve God, rejoicing in the power of the Holy Spirit. Amen.

Permission is granted for the leader to copy this page for distribution to the participants in the group.

Course Evaluation

Help us assess the value of this course and plan for future programs in this area by completing this evaluation. Thank you.

1. This course met my expectations.

    ___ yes ___ no ___ partially ___ I had no expectations

    Additional comments:

2. I have a sense of direction for keeping my life together now.

    ___ yes ___ no ___ some ___ I am not looking for a sense of direction.

    Additional comments:

3. An important learning for me from this course was:

4. Whatever you want the leaders to know:

"Bear with One Another" (Col. 3:13)

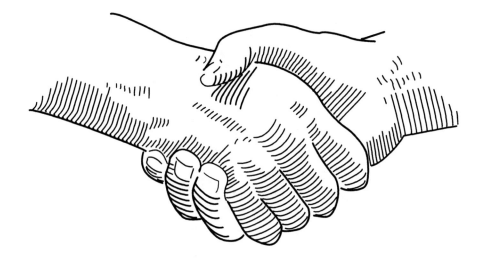

Notes

Introduction

1. Marjorie Thompson, *Family the Forming Center* (Nashville: Upper Room Books, 1996), 14.

Chapter 1

1. Patrick Miller, *Deuteronomy,* Interpretation (Atlanta: John Knox Press, 1990), 241–45.
2. M. Scott Peck, *The Road Less Traveled* (New York: Simon and Schuster, 1978), 65, 67.
3. Diana R. Garland, "Focusing Families: Reflections on Genesis 2:7–3:13," *Journal of Family Ministry* 10, no. 3 (Winter 1996): 27–33.

Chapter 2

1. Tilden Edwards, *Sabbath Time* (Nashville: Upper Room Books, 1992), 148–49.

Chapter 3

1. Douglas R. A. Hare, *Matthew,* Interpretation (Louisville, Ky.: John Knox Press, 1993), 153–54.
2. Tilden Edwards, *Sabbath Time* (Nashville: Upper Room Books, 1992), 101–33.

3. Delia Halverson, *Living Simply, Simply Living* (Nashville: Abingdon Press, 1996), 18.
4. Marjorie Thompson, *Family the Forming Center* (Nashville: Upper Room Books, 1996), 61.
5. Ibid., 59.
6. From personal correspondence with Bonnie Michaels, Managing Work & Family, Inc.

Chapter 4

1. Bonnie Michaels and Elizabeth McCarty, *Solving the Work/Family Puzzle,* (Homewood, Ill.: Business One Irwin, 1992), 106.
2. Roberta C. Bondi, "When We Can't Seem to Pray," *Weavings,* vol. 8, no. 5 (September/October 1998): 29.

Chapter 5

1. Ralph Martin, *Colossians,* Interpretation (Atlanta: John Knox Press, 1991), 125.
2. Ernest Boyer, Jr., *A Way in the World: Family Life as Spiritual Discipline* (San Francisco: Harper & Row, 1984), 103–5.

Bibliography

Boyer, Ernest, Jr. *A Way in the World: Family Life as Spiritual Discipline.* San Francisco: Harper & Row, 1984.

Edwards, Tilden. *Sabbath Time.* Nashville: Upper Room Books, 1992.

Halverson, Delia. *Living Simply, Simply Living.* Nashville: Abingdon Press, 1996.

Hickman, Martha Whitmore. *A Day of Rest,* Creating a Spiritual Space in Your Week. New York: Avon Books, 1999.

Linn, Dennis; Sheila Fabricant Linn; and Matthew Linn. *Sleeping with Bread, Holding What Gives You Life.* New York: Paulist Press, 1995.

Michaels, Bonnie, and Elizabeth McCarty. *Solving the Work/ Family Puzzle.* Homewood, Ill.: Business One Irwin, 1992.

Miller-McLemore, Bonnie. *Also a Mother: Work and Family as Theological Dilemma.* Nashville: Abingdon Press, 1994.

Olson, Richard P., and Joe H. Leonard Jr. *A New Day for Family Ministry.* Washington, D.C.: Alban Institute, 1996.

Payden, Deborah Alberswerth, and Laura Loving. *Celebrating at*

Home: Prayers and Liturgies for Families. Cleveland: United Church Press, 1998.

Sine, Tom. *Live It Up! How to Create a Life You Can Love*. Scottdale, Pa.: Herald Press, 1993.

Thompson, Marjorie, *Family the Forming Center: A Vision of the Role of Family in Spiritual Formation*. Nashville: Upper Room Books, 1996.

———. *Soul Feast*. Louisville, Ky.: Westminster John Knox Press, 1995.

Weavings, 1908 Grand Avenue, P.O. Box 189, Nashville, TN 37202-0189.

LINCOLN CHRISTIAN UNIVERSITY 126409

CPSIA information can be obtained at www.ICGtesting.com
Printed in the USA
LVOW111022300912

300896LV00005B/60/P

3 4711 00211 4405